What Belongs to God

Reflections on Peacemaking by a Conscientious Objector

David Livingston Edwards

To learn more about this book and its author, please visit
WhatBelongsToGod.com

Cover design and illustration by Rick Nease
www.RickNeaseArt.com

Published by
Front Edge Publishing
42807 Ford Road, Suite 234
Canton, MI, 48187

Front Edge Publishing books are available for discount bulk purchases for
events, corporate use and small groups. Special editions, including books with
corporate logos, personalized covers and customized interiors are available
for purchase. For more information, contact Front Edge Publishing at info@
FrontEdgePublishing.com

This book is dedicated to our children,
Kent Edwards and Shelley Edwards
and all others who continue to work for
peace and justice in this country and beyond.

Contents

Praise for *What Belongs to God*

The two great problems of our society are a lack of conscience and the intentional violence towards those we have rendered socially invisible. David Edwards in these pages renders a powerful moral critique of these two problems and calls readers to maintain their commitment to nonviolence, love and truth.

The Rev. Dr. William J. Barber II, president of Repairers of the Breach and co-chair of the Poor People's Campaign

What Belongs to God is a testimony that will inspire another generation to find the courage to value all life. There is so much in this book. It is a manual on character, a guide to decision-making, a testimony to the cause of justice and an affirmation of the dedication to serving one's brother and sister in love.

Shaykh Ahmed Abdur Rashid, founder of The World Community spiritual center in Virginia

This book is a wonderful articulation of the spiritual basis of nonviolence. It provided words for some of the spiritual convictions I have held but never have been able to explain adequately.

Janaki Spickard Keeler, coordinator of pamphlets at Pendle Hill Quaker center

In clear, uncomplicated language, David Edwards takes us on his own life journey following the path of Jesus as peacemaker. As he examines the gospel accounts, he uncovers for readers many meanings or subtleties that go beyond surface understandings. Being a peacemaker in the following of Jesus may be more costly and more inconvenient than one might have imagined. The reader who takes the journey with David Edward will be surprised and challenged.

Sister Elaine Prevallet, Sister of Loretto and author of *Reflections on Simplicity*

David Edwards doesn't simply tell a beautiful story in this book, he also provides an inspiring witness to the power and inspiration of one person standing on principles and values against the odds. Those of us who knew him will never cease to be challenged by memories of his uncompromising faithfulness, matched only by an abiding sadness that he is no longer with us.

The Rev. Dr. Jan G. Linn, author of *Unbinding Christianity, Choosing the Values of Jesus over the Beliefs of the Church*

It would be difficult to find a more heartfelt, articulate and personal piece of writing focused on the issues surrounding the experience of being a Christian conscientious objector in our society. David Edwards' *What Belongs to God* speaks to innumerable facets of this important and nuanced topic. He offers a thorough discussion of Biblical quotes and interpretations and speaks of the passionate conviction of his heart's calling to honor God and care for others. By turns uplifting and sobering, David walks the reader through the philosophical and religious challenges he encountered in response to his stance. And he gives us a beautiful view into his years as a nurse's aide in a Boston children's cardiac unit, his civilian alternative service. He shares the sometimes-forceful objections he heard from congregants during his many years in ministry. There's so much to learn here. Open your heart and read carefully.

Elizabeth Heaney, MA LPC, author of *The Honor Was Mine*

In times of enduring warfare—and war metaphors for addressing pandemics, climate change and poverty—David Edwards offers a biblically grounded and theologically insightful testimony about what it means to live non-violently for the sake of creation. He invites us on a transformative journey toward peace as we practice nonviolence in a country with the largest military power in human history.

The Rev. Dr. Rita Nakashima Brock, co-author of *Saving Paradise: How Christianity Traded Love of This World for Crucifixion and Empire*

David Edwards brings his personal experience and profound exegesis of core Bible passages together to address questions that every young person, indeed every Christian, should be asking themselves in these times of American empire. His thoughtful responses to the radical demands of the Prophets and the Gospel bring much light to bear on the matter of discipleship. This is a beautiful account of his journey to ethical maturity.

The Rev. Dr. Dick Hamm, former General Minister and President of the Christian Church (Disciples of Christ) in the U.S. and Canada

We can read the title of David Edwards' memoir *What Belongs to God* as either a statement or a question. In this heartfelt and personal reliving of his journey as a conscientious objector, Edwards leaves no doubt about his answer: Everything belongs to God. Edwards' life story brings alive the biblical and theological plea to offer our total allegiance to God and thus know, "a universal and compelling Love that is nonviolent at its core." This book is an important contribution to a conversation all too frequently muted.

The Rev. Dr. Sharon E. Watkins, former General Minister and President, Christian Church (Disciples of Christ)

The Draft: An Objection

These are the young men who swam
in pools of boyhood, whose hands I held,
who launched paper kites into April skies,
who march before you now.
And you inspect their groins
like so many rifle barrels,
you who take the measure
of their manhood
with a bloodied flag.

These are the young men
who listened to your fables,
told with silver tongue,
which wooed them into hell.
They were shattered in their tracks
and sent home in pieces,
stitched together with ribbons,
medals, and your words, those curious,
hollow words you rattle in my face
as you ask me why it is
I would not go with them.

Foreword

Everyone has a right to live—and every life belongs to God!

In short, this is the thesis so carefully unpacked by David Edwards in *What Belongs to God: Reflections of a Conscientious Objector*. In this brief work, David describes his decision to peacefully resist the Vietnam War.

So much more than a memoir of a moment in time, *What Belongs to God* illustrates the significance of baring one's soul to the Ultimate Power of Love; the impact this primary connection has on all other connections.

> *"If we take our religious faith seriously enough to live with it over time, there grows in the heart and mind the sense of a Power and Presence infusing the whole of life, the love of which makes all other loyalties or allegiances of secondary value."*

David's moral compass was set under the life-long tutelage of his faith community—one of the earliest influences being his father (my friend and mentor) the Rev. Barney P. Edwards. The elder Edwards served in ministry in Virginia concurrent with my ministry there. Having shared this bit of spiritual lineage, I still found myself being pushed, pulled and prodded by David's words to think more deeply about what it means to be faithful.

I was particularly struck by his exegesis of the Genesis account of Cain's slaying of Abel, his brother. David lifts up the famous phrase, "Am I my brother's keeper?" In examining the Hebrew word for "keeper" ("keeper" in Hebrew is attributed to God alone) David argues Cain is guilty not simply of killing his brother. Deeper than that—morally and spiritually—Cain was "playing God" with his brother's life. We are *not* our brother's "keeper." We are our brother's *brother*.

> *"Keeping another human being has to do with not only the act of killing but also any act or way of thinking that deprives others of their access to life."*

If the moral questions raised by the Vietnam War seem distant to today's challenges, one need only reflect on any of a number of current events that plague us today to find the relevance of David's posthumously published wisdom.

My own journey has been marked by such pivotal encounters, not the least of which came when Bishop William J. Barber, II called me to be part of the growing movement to work with and walk beside the 140 million poor and low wealth people in this country. Would I lend my voice and passion to address the five interlocking evils and injustices of our day: systemic racism, systemic poverty, ecological devastation, the war biased economy and the false moral narrative of religious nationalism was indeed a call from God? My faith said, "Yes." My feet have followed.

David's words affirm the call (mine as well as yours) to resist lesser allegiances; to live as though we believe everyone has a right to live— and every life belongs to God!

Thank you, David, for illustrating not just with these words, but with your entire life, the humility *and* priceless nature of our humanity.

Rev. Dr. Alvin O'Neal Jackson
National Executive Director
Mass Poor People's Assembly and Moral March on Washington
Poor People's Campaign: A National Call for Moral Revival

Come Sing With Me: An Introduction to David Edwards Through His Music

I hope you enjoy meeting David through a few of the many songs he composed. Every verse and refrain below is available as a free download at WhatBelongsToGod.com. Recordings of David's original singing are also available on the site. See a song's attribution for the name of the CD, the track number and the direct link.

David and I were married on Christmas Day in 1969 in the middle of our senior year of college. Shortly after graduation in the spring of 1970 we moved to Boston, MA for David to serve his two years of alternative service as a conscientious objector to the draft. We both worked at Boston Children's Hospital. This love song, "Pine Forest Floor," is one of several that David wrote to me over the 50 years of our marriage. It was composed to celebrate our first wedding anniversary, spent at a friend's rustic cabin in Vermont.

"Pine Forest Floor"
Free as the branches caressing the sky,
Warm as the earth when winter's gone by.

WHAT BELONGS TO GOD

I'll give you your ease and we'll be what we'll be
As we lie in the arms of a pine forest floor.

(A Different Kind of Strength, track #2)
whatbelongstogod.com/music/DK-Pine.mp3

After the two years in Boston, we moved to Lexington, KY where we both attended seminary, adopted our son Kent, and two months later our daughter Shelley was born. David began his first pastorate in Lexington in 1974. He wrote many liturgical songs, hymns and psalm responses during his long service as a local pastor. His music, like all of his writings, is often challenging to conventional ways of thinking about the Bible and what it means to be a Christian. One example I especially like, "The Greatest Things," was written in these early years.

"The Greatest Things"
The greatest things in the world are the things you cannot own.
The greatest things in the world are always there
when you think you're all alone.

(A Different Kind of Strength, track #6)
whatbelongstogod.com/music/DK-Greatest.mp3

David was most comfortable confronting injustice through his sermon writing, his music and later in life through his blog, *The View from Here*. Yet he always felt that writing wasn't enough and he pushed himself to get involved in social justice activities. This was quite the challenge for an extreme introvert. During his first pastorate, he learned of the housing inequality in Lexington, KY, and met many good people caught up in this inequity. This song, "Don't Weep for Delores," shows his deep compassion for others and his lifelong commitment to confronting issues of injustice, even when it made him uncomfortable.

"Don't Weep for Delores"
She lived in the caverns of the city
In the shadow of wealth without pity.
In a hovel so cold it would soon freeze the soul of Delores.

Delores,
Don't weep for Delores,
She has gone. She has gone before us
To a land that is free
No more misery for Delores.

(A Different Kind of Strength, track #7)
whatbelongstogod.com/music/DK-Delores.mp3

When our children were 2 and 3 years old we moved back to Lynchburg, VA, where we had both graduated college. We continued to live there through our children's growing-up years. Once, while the children and I were away, David missed us terribly and wrote this song, "I have Four Gifts for You." The song was written in one sitting and sung at a concert later that same day. His composing often happened in this manner.

"I Have Four Gifts for You"

I have four gifts for you, my child. I have four gifts for you.
They're all that I can give, my child. So precious and so few.

I give you April's flower, my child ...
I give you summer's green, my child ...
October is a gift, my child, wrapped in a fiery hue ...
I give to you a season, child, so cold and white and drear ...
Hold close to you these gifts, my child and well they will keep
you.

(A Different Kind of Strength, track #5)
whatbelongstogod.com/music/DK-Gifts.mp3

After our first experience serving different churches during our seminary years, we decided we would never do that again and we didn't. For the first few years that David served as the minister of the Lynchburg First Christian Church (Disciples of Christ), I worked as the children's advocate at a shelter for abused women and as a counselor for a local family service organization. As time passed I had the opportunity to work with David as the associate minister. These were exciting and difficult years. We felt called to lead the church to do some rather uncomfortable things, such as allowing demonstrations on the front lawn of the church whenever a death sentence was carried out by the state of Virginia, reaching out to individuals and families suffering from the AIDS epidemic, and being very public about our welcoming people of all sexual orientations. We also had many personal challenges during these years. In addition to raising two strong-willed teenagers in the very public life of a minister's family, I experienced several serious health problems, and both of David's parents and my father died. Still, David continued to write and perform during this period. It was impossible to choose just one song that captures these tumultuous, yet prolific years, so I chose two. "And Now He's Gone," was written to honor David's father.

> *"And Now He's Gone"*
>
> *His hands were strong to fell a tree,*
> *or build most anything;*
> *but gentle as he penned the words*
> *to soothe the heart that's grieving,*
> *or stroke the string of fiddle or harp*
> *for music soft and fine.*
> *And now he's gone,*
> *glad I am to feel his hands in mine.*
>
> *(A Different Kind of Strength, track #9)*
> *whatbelongstogod.com/music/DK-Gone.mp3*

The Psalms were always part of David's daily meditation practice. Putting the words of a psalm to music comforted him and brought him closer to God, especially during difficult times.

> *"In Peace I Lie Down and Sleep"*
> *Psalm 4*
>
> *In peace I lie down and sleep.*
> *For the Lord makes me dwell in safety.*
> *Answer me when I call, O God of my right!*
> *You have given me room when I was in distress.*
> *Be gracious to me, be gracious to me,*

and hear my prayer.

(I Will Praise God as Long as I Live, track #13)
whatbelongstogod.com/music/PG-Sleep.mp3

In 1995, after 15 years in Lynchburg, we moved to Indianapolis, IN, so that I could accept a call as the Director of Children and Family Ministries with the General Offices of the Christian Church (Disciples of Christ). This job gave us the opportunity to travel. We went to South Africa for the World AIDS Conference and to India with a group of United Church of Christ and Disciples clergy. During these years I kept David quite busy writing songs for me to use in my work for the denomination. He wrote songs for vacation Bible school programs and for national gatherings. "Children Welcome" (*What Will We Say to the Children?* track #8: *whatbelongstogod.com/music/ WW-Children.mp3*) is still used by many Disciples churches to call their children forward for a children's sermon. David composed "We Will Arise," for a General Assembly AIDS healing service.

"We Will Arise"

We will arise on healing wings
Through clouds of sorrow
Through storms of pain;
for now we know that death and dread
no more can hold us, we will arise.

(Arabella's Eyes, track #8)
whatbelongstogod.com/music/AE-Arise.mp3

While I worked at the denominational headquarters in Indianapolis, we lived in a small town just east of the city where David served a Disciples congregation. In all honesty, this was David's most difficult pastorate. During the 1990s, there was talk of the draft being reinstituted, so David wrote up a document to help congregations to talk with their youth about the option of conscientious objection. The leaders of this church refused to let him share the document, believing it to be "unpatriotic." A free packet on conscientious objection, that David put together, can be obtained through The Disciples Peace Fellowship

at https://www.disciplespeace.org. It seems appropriate to share one
of his many songs about peacemaking with you.

"Blessed Are the Peacemakers"

Blessed are the peacemakers. You must love your enemy.
Sell all you have to help the poor, and come follow me.
This is the way that Jesus lived, the words that he did say
And those who want to follow him will live the same way.

(Arabella's Eyes, track #5)

whatbelongstogod.com/music/AE-Peacemakers.mp3

After eight years in Indiana we moved back to Lynchburg, VA,
where David had accepted a call to the Church of the Covenant, a
small church modeled after the Church of the Savior in Washington
D.C. and affiliated with the United Church of Christ. He continued
to write a great deal of music during this time and produced a third
book of songs.

It is ironic that his pastoral ministry began and ended in small
churches that hired him because he was a CO, not in spite of it. This
last church, the Church of the Covenant, was and continues to be a
congregation that is serious about the balance between one's prayer
life and one's involvement in social action. They frame the Christian
life as an inward and outward journey. "Morning Song" is a beautiful
picture of David's inward journey. He spent each and every morning
of his life in the way this song describes.

"Morning Song"

Morning comes quietly dawning.
Light slowly grows on the hills.
Earth makes its turning around the great sun,
my spirit its turning to God.

Before I go out to my labors,
receiving the gift of the day.
I sit in the silence and listen within
to a voice calling softly to me.

(I Will Praise God as Long as I Live, track #1)
whatbelongstogod.com/music/PG-Morning.mp3

In retirement, David's life work of making peace turned to singing with children in a local Head Start program. He wrote a number of songs to help children notice and connect to the natural beauty around them. "The Dragonfly Song" was one of his favorites. He loved the mythology and symbolism attached to dragonflies and, shortly before retiring, had one tattooed on the inside of his right arm.

"Dragonfly Song"

Have you seen a dragonfly?
Do you know what she can do?
She can fly forward, and fly back.
She can fly up, and then fly down.
And sometimes all she wants to do
is stop and look around.

(Songs for Children, track #1)
whatbelongstogod.com/music/SC-Dragonfly.mp3

Just a few short years after retiring, David was diagnosed with esophageal cancer in 2018. The cancer had already spread to other organs and he lived only one year after the diagnosis. "This Body is Clay," written many years earlier, was inspired by a conversation with a close minister friend. At the celebration of life services, which the children and I planned, we sang many of his songs, but we listened to him sing this one.

"This Body is Clay"

This body is clay; it won't last forever.
My days are few and precious spent
And when I die, lord, lord,
lay me down in peace,
and I'll be satisfied, and I'll be content.

(A Different Kind of Strength, track #10)
whatbelongstogod.com/music/DK-Clay.mp3

May it be so.

Meet the Author in Photographs

David spends time with his granddaughter. (2015)

The Boston years. (1970-1972)

A trip to India. (2002)

David and Kaye Edwards conducting his
niece's wedding. (early 2000)

The whole family at the beach. (2018)

Singing with children at Camp Kum-ba-yah,
Lynchburg, VA. (2015)

From the Author

In the culture of the United States, joining the military forces is taken for granted as a morally unquestionable matter. This has been true from the time of the invasion and conquering of North America by white Europeans to the present day. Military service continues to be touted as the highest form of service to one's country, if not to humanity. Churches, pacifist groups and individuals opposing participation in the military always have been relatively small in number and visibility. Though generally tolerated, they also have been met with hostility and, in some cases, violence. We are increasingly a nationalistic and militaristic culture within which the only positive moral response to military enlistment presented to young people is to join up and do one's duty. By nationalistic I mean an excessive love for one's own country, to the point of seeing it as exceptional, even superior, in relation to other countries. Militarism is the glorification and promotion of participation in the military as the highest, even exclusive, form of service to one's country. It includes the uncritical support of military actions and involvements judged to be in the interest of one's own country.

In the spring of 1970, I was approved by my local Selective Service, or draft board, as a conscientious objector (CO), designated I-O, unwilling to serve in the military in a non-combatant capacity. I performed the required two-year civilian alternative service at Boston (MA) Children's Hospital Medical Center from 1970–72. My decision to refuse military service was a direct outgrowth of my religious upbringing and studies. As a Christian, my moral sense was shaped by the teachings and life of Jesus. The reality of the war in Vietnam, and my decision with regard to it, confronted me in the inescapable form of the draft lottery. My number was 16, thus immediately making me vulnerable to call-up. By then I was clear about what my decision would be. Jesus taught nonviolence and love of enemies, manifesting this in his life and death. As a follower of Jesus, I could not participate in a human institution the core purpose of which was to kill other human beings in the name of and for the ambitions of my country.

My decision as a conscientious objector flowed naturally from my religious tradition, which I had internalized and deepened in my mind and heart. For me, there simply was no choice: To join the military with a willingness to fight and kill those identified as my enemies was morally wrong. It conflicted with my spiritual understanding and inward sense of what it means to be a human being. However, I soon found out that my view of things was not widely shared in church or society. I encountered ambivalence from some who held me in high esteem and lent their support yet found my decision somewhat misguided. They thought that nonviolence and love of enemies were lofty ideals, but that there are times when we must be willing to fight against those who mean harm to others, us or our way of life. My decision put me on a collision course with many whose responses were unambivalent. I was often regarded with hostility and anger from those for whom military service to the nation was near and dear, in spite of what Jesus taught or did. Some of this, of course, came from those who had been in the military. I must say, however, that there were a few in the churches I later served who had seen combat in Vietnam and were quite supportive, understanding and even appreciative of my position. As one congregant, who had served as a combat officer in the war, told me, "If anyone gives you a problem, send them to me." Though the church had nurtured and nourished in me a deep commitment to the peace-filled teachings of Jesus, the church generally seemed either uneasy with or hostile toward those who took such teachings to heart when it came to participation in the military. During that time of decision, I began to find my strongest support and companionship among those outside of the church.

In later years, my reflections and studies have helped me see that what I experienced reflected a tension within the Hebrew and Christian scriptures themselves. Yet, it is not a tension belonging exclusively to the Jewish/Christian tradition. The message and messengers of the major religions taught and lived peacefulness and nonviolence, including some form of loving one's enemies. However, in practice there often has been animosity toward those not of one's own religion or nation. Room is always reserved for what is judged to be justifiable violence. There is, I believe, a core morality in Hebrew and Christian scriptures that bends decidedly toward the nonviolent life and a love that embraces the stranger, including one's enemy. Though this morality of nonviolence is at the heart of my spiritual tradition, it does not dominate the life, thoughts or actions of the majority of its adherents when it comes to war and the military. This reality does not diminish the truth-claim of our scriptural teachings on peace, nonviolence and compassionate love for all. This is especially true when it comes to the words and life of Jesus as presented in the four gospels. There certainly are voices in our scriptures that support violence, justified by religious laws or the will of God as understood by God's people in certain situations. These are part of a minor scriptural strain that is in opposition to and negated by a dominant essential message: We are, as humans created by God, meant for peaceable lives and not for killing one another. This is our nature as God's children, and it is always the sacred vision and dream for our lives. We are capable of and constrained to live this kind of life. Only such a life fulfills who we are, as individuals and as a human family. Though the nonviolent life is that for which we were created, it is always something we are free to choose or reject. That is the choice out of which this book arose and about which I am chiefly concerned.

In some of the following chapters, I share my own story as a con-scientious objector—how my decision developed, my experience of civilian alternative service in a hospital for children, and my life and work as a pastor and conscientious objector. Other chapters explore the core scriptural teachings that have formed my own life, beliefs and actions as a CO. A chapter is devoted to those portions of Jesus' life and teachings which have been misread and employed in the effort to make room for violence on the part of Christians. I will not attempt a full-scale treatment of the entirety of the Bible. Yet, there are par-ticular portions of scripture that stand out with regard to nonviolent living. Some are stories. Some are teachings. All were potent factors in shaping my decision with regard to military service. I believe they need to be listened to and addressed by anyone who is considering participation in the military, especially one who considers himself or herself a follower of Jesus.

The issue of military service as a moral decision must be consid-ered not only by individuals within the Christian Church but also by the church itself and its leaders. This needs to be done openly in an atmosphere of respectfulness, with no violent speech or actions. Such would not be an easy or painless experience. There are many in the churches who are attached to the value of military service, who have experienced profound trauma because of their participation in warfare, and some who have lost friends or family members in combat. Still, we cannot shy away from difficult discussions because some of us are hurt or angry. At stake is what it means to be communities and individuals who follow Jesus, who take his moral teachings seriously, who know that we are loved unconditionally by God. We are called to live the kind of life God created us to live, as revealed in the life and teachings of Jesus.

What I write is meant for all people, not just those within my own religious tradition. Jesus' life and teachings are not for one certain group of people or even for one religion, but for all humanity. The life of nonviolence, refusing to kill, forgiving one's enemies, is the life for which we are all made. It is who we really and truly are. Religion, at its best, is not about some life beyond this one. It is about how best

to live this life, on this Earth, with and among those who are part
of the human family, near and far. In my experience as a conscientious objector, I have met those committed to nonviolence and love
of enemies who are Christian, Jewish, Muslim, Buddhist, as well as
those who claim no religious tradition. These are all, to my mind and
heart, the true human family, seeking to live harmoniously with what
we call God—the Presence and Power from which and to which all
life flows, and by which all of life is sustained.

A final word about language. I use the word *God* symbolically. It
points to a Reality permeating all of life, as the Source and Power
of Life itself. In recent decades, theology is finding a new voice with
which to speak, one that takes seriously our scientific understanding
of the universe, how it works, and our part and place in that universe
as human beings. The notion of a *God up there* who breaks into our
lives as humans to influence and direct events can no longer hold. I
do not believe in God as a celestial *person* or deity, but as a Power
and Presence pervading all of life and with which we as humans must
harmonize our living. If we do not do so, the results are harmful for
us and for the creation of which we are part. If we do, the harvest is
fulfillment, peace, justice and abundance for all, what the Bible calls
salvation or the *kingdom of God*. I will use theological language found
in the scriptures, and yet will attempt to do so in ways that reflect a
more current understanding of life and its relationship to the Sacred.

My CO Story Begins

In the winter and spring of 1970, I applied to the Selective Service System as a conscientious objector (CO) to war in any form, based on my religious beliefs. Nothing I have heard, read or seen since then has modified that decision. My objection to war and participation in the military, though gradual in its unfolding, came with complete clarity. Certainly, there have been many times when I have re-examined and been questioned about that decision. However, I have always returned to the fundamental conviction that I am not created to kill or be part of killing, whether in a uniform or not. I believe this to be true for all human beings. Recent events in our country, acts of war and the uprising of the militaristic and nationalistic spirit, have led me once more to revisit my life as one who has grown increasingly wary of that spirit.

I grew up in a moderate Protestant Christian tradition. My father was a minister in the Christian Church (Disciples of Christ), and his spiritual influence on me was that of tolerance, peaceableness and a religious faith open to learning and questioning. My experience of the church was largely positive. I felt loved and cared for, as well as encouraged to grow in my understanding of the scriptures and Christian life. I don't recall there being a predominance of what is called atonement theology, that God sent Jesus to die for our sins, that we are to believe in Jesus so that we will be saved from this life and have a place in heaven. Such a theological view was certainly present. It was in many of the hymns we sang and prayers that were said. After all, I grew up in the so-called Bible Belt. My own denomination, however, had a strong emphasis on the importance of having an informed and maturing faith. This resulted in a more positive view of human life and a greater emphasis on Christian discipleship, that is, being a follower of Jesus. More attention was given to Jesus' life and teachings and what they meant for the way I lived. I loved the readings from the Sermon on the Mount and other ethical teachings. The parables caught my attention because they made me think and rethink the way I understood life and lived it. The passion and death of Jesus became central to my faith, not because of the *Jesus-died-on-the-cross-to-save-me-from-my-sins* theology, but because of what I saw as Jesus' total devotion to the way of love. That commitment to a greater reality and truth ran counter to the religious and political powers of his day, resulting in his death. The resurrection simply meant that God's power of love was greater than the pretending, illusory powers of human making.

I also grew up in a culture saturated with love of nation and the military. The highest, noblest form of commitment was to military service. My high school years coincided with a dawning awareness of our involvement in Vietnam. This was also a time of the fresh-faced national enthusiasm accompanying John F. Kennedy and his "Camelot" administration. We were in Vietnam to save a country from communism, and to stop a "domino effect" of Southeast Asian nations falling, one by one, to an atheistic political movement determined to take over the world. I was in Boy Scouts for a while, partaking of the cozy blend of nationalism and soft-core militarism. I even earned my "God and Country" award at a time before I understood that there might be tension between the two.

My first wake-up call came unexpectedly one day as I sat in a high school social studies class. It was taught by Mr. Clarence Parker, who was progressive and challenging. One day, he led us in a discussion of the war in Vietnam, whether or not we supported it and why. I spoke right up, saying that if our president thought we should be there, then we should support him and his policies. The words came out of me as something parroted and not really believed. Mr. Parker pushed his glasses up on the bridge of his nose, then said wryly, "You mean our country right or wrong, eh, Mr. Edwards?" Immediately I felt my face flush and sweat beading on my forehead. No, I said inside myself, that's not what I meant. That, however, was exactly what I had said. From that moment I began to think seriously about my faith in relation to national politics and policy, especially regarding war. That small interchange became a decisive turning point in my thinking and my life direction.

The Selective Service System had a set of classifications for draft-age men. I entered Lynchburg College, a small central Virginia liberal arts college, planning on entering the ministry. As a pre-ministerial student, I was given a IV-D exemption, which was valid as long as I finished undergraduate studies and went on to seminary. My college was founded by and related to the Disciples of Christ denomination, and had a history of preparing many of its students for ministry. I came to campus full of religious zeal and found myself among a small group of like-minded pre-ministerial students. It was in this way I met Kaye Talbot Speakes, who would eventually become my wife and partner in the conscientious objector process.

Over the course of the first semester and into the second, I began to chafe under my "divine" exemption from the decisions and fates being faced by my other male contemporaries. I also was chafing under the whole religious "thing," gradually drifting away from the pre-ministerial fellowship. This was a turning away from my church background and toward a more secular life and view. I found myself breaking out of a shell into a world richly colored by my readings of Camus, Thoreau and the English romantic poets. I experienced a growing thirst for music of all kinds, especially the flourishing folk scene. At the same time, I was turning toward a more serious study of theology, particularly the writings and life of Dietrich Bonhoeffer. Bonhoeffer was a German theologian and pastor martyred by the

Nazis in April 1945 for his part in the underground resistance and the plot against Hitler's life. His theme of "costly discipleship" rang a bell deep in my soul, the idea that God's love for us, manifested in Jesus, calls for a life of radical discipleship to him and faithfulness to his teachings.

My mind was turning to my own life and the looming storm of the war that was claiming the lives of more and more young U.S. citizens and countless citizens of a country on the far side of the world. My first step toward objection seemed to make itself. One day I drove downtown to the Selective Service office, walked in, and announced to a bewildered secretary at the front desk that I wished to drop my IV-D exemption. She looked up at me with genuine concern and asked, "You know what this means?"

"Yes," I said. I was re-classified II-S, which meant that as a college student my availability for the draft was deferred until I either graduated or quit school. I left the office with a heady feeling of having acted in accord with something at the core of my being. I also felt anxious because I did not know what the next step would be or what lay ahead. I was sharing the uneasiness felt by most young men my age during those years—the inevitability of military conscription into a devastating, immoral war. It was a confusing and frightening time. However, my decision was becoming increasingly clear as one who, though now unchurched, as it were, still understood himself as a follower of Jesus. Over the next two years, my way ahead gradually came into focus.

My Brother's/Sister's Keeper?

When I finished my two years of alternative service, I entered graduate studies at Lexington Theological Seminary in Kentucky. I became fascinated with Hebrew scriptures (the Old Testament) because of the young professor Dr. George W. Coats. I was attracted by his stellar scholarship that he blended with his warm and open humanity. The class I remember most clearly was on the first 11 chapters of the Book of Genesis. This portion is known as *primeval history*, stories relating to the earliest times. Such literature is "story," not scientific history as we tend to think of it. And it was from Dr. Coats that I learned the difference between story truth and scientific or historical truth. The Greek word for story is *muthos*, or myth. We are wrong when we use "myth" to mean something that is not true. We need myths or stories that express our understanding of ourselves as human beings and our place in the universe. Certainly, some myths wither away and new ones arise. What I learned in the study of the stories in Genesis 1-11 was the genius and depth of insight and truth of ancient people who predated the history of the Patriarchs, which begins with Abraham (Genesis 12). For me, one of the foremost of those stories was that of Cain's killing of his brother, Abel (Genesis 4).

Like to most Christians, as well as many non-Christians, the story of Cain and Abel is familiar mainly because of the famous response Cain gives to God, "Am I my brother's keeper?" This occurs after Cain has killed his brother out of a fit of jealous rage. He did it because God, for some unknown reason, was pleased with Abel's sacrifice of one of his flock, but not with Cain's offering of something from "the fruit of the ground." Cain was a gardener; Abel was a shepherd. Farmers and ranchers—an ancient rivalry. However, the reason for Cain's killing of his brother is not the focal point of the story. Cain felt unjustly treated. In his view, the world hadn't done him right. So, he lashed out. He let his emotions get the best of him and, in a cloud of rage and jealousy, chose to take his brother's life.

The story then centers on Cain's response to God: "Am I my brother's keeper?" Like most people, I thought for many years that the answer was, "Yes, of course you are your brother's keeper." You are supposed to care about and take care of your brother, not kill him. That answer, I learned, is both right and wrong. Right in that Cain should not have killed his brother. Wrong regarding what it means to be the keeper of another human being. Dr. Coats had assigned us an essay by Paul A. Riemann, then at Drew University, titled "Am I My Brother's Keeper?" (*Interpretation*, October 1970). Professor Riemann's thesis was that this very familiar story is misunderstood and misinterpreted. The answer to Cain's question is no. He is *not* his brother's "keeper." Why? Because the Hebrew word for "keeper" is used only in reference to God in the Hebrew scriptures. God alone is the "keeper" of human beings. We need only reference the beloved Psalm 121, in which the words "keep" and "keeper" occur six times, always describing God's care of us human beings.

Then what is going on in this story? We thought it was an open-and-shut case of Cain's being guilty of NOT being his brother's keeper. What I learned from looking again at this famed story, in light of Professor Riemann's article, caused something of a seismic shift within me. Cain was indeed guilty of killing his brother. Yet the truth of what that killing meant was radically deepened, morally and spiritually. Cain was guilty precisely of playing God with his brother's life.

He had *kept* his brother in the ultimate sense by robbing him of his life. This meaning is intensified by another detail in the story. When Cain gives God what we now see as a smart-aleck response to God's inquiry as to the whereabouts of his brother God knows right away what has happened. God fires back: "What have you done?" Then God orders Cain to "… listen; your brother's blood is crying out to me from the ground!" Abel's blood, as well as our own, belongs to God alone. Humans may be the keepers of flocks and herds. However, they do not belong to each other in such a way as to have any right of control over, much less killing, one another. God orders Cain and orders us to listen to the blood of our sisters and brothers crying out to God.

I had not had this deeper understanding of the Cain and Abel story during the earlier time of my objection to military service. Yet when I studied this story in that seminary class it resounded within my mind and soul. I recognized that this was exactly what I understood back then about the nature of killing, including the killing legitimized by the military and nation in war. It was such a profound sense of the nature of things that I could not fully articulate it. To take another human being's life, whether wearing a uniform or not, is keeping the life of a brother or sister in the ultimate sense. It is taking the place of God. All of the rationalizations, all of the reasons given for why one should be willing to kill, evaporated in the face of this one clear and profound truth: I am not the keeper of my brother or sister whose blood belongs only to God and not to me. The ancient story spoke to me of the essential nature of life, my own life and that of others, something that cannot be transgressed without severe consequences. This is reaffirmed at the end of the story when God puts a "mark" on Cain. It is not a curse, but a protective mark so that no human being might take vengeance upon Cain. Even the blood of Cain the killer, the murderer, belongs ineradicably to God.

Each life belongs to the Source of Life, which we call God. Here is the foundation of what Dr. Albert Schweitzer called having and living with a "reverence for life." It is the foundation of Mohandas Gandhi's *ahimsa*, or "not harming." And it is at the core of the biblical

understanding of life in both Hebrew and Christian scriptures. The
Cain and Abel story gives us a significant and vivid image for this: We
are not the "keepers" of one another. We cannot insert ourselves into
the sacred relationship between God and any human life. Gandhi and
Schweitzer, however, would include all sentient life forms.

"Keeping" another human being has to do with not only the act of
killing but also any act or way of thinking that deprives others of their
access to life. European peoples invading North America, commit-
ting genocide against the native people of this land, as well as stealing
and "reeducating" their children—this is keeping. Forcibly removing
African people from their countries, bringing hundreds of thousands
to this country to live, work and die enslaved, creating wealth for
white people—this is keeping. Rechanneling poisoned water into
the town of Flint, Michigan, sickening and threatening the lives of
its residents—this is keeping. Political maneuvering to rob people of
their right to vote, thus their voice in determining their own lives—
this is keeping. The emotional, sexual and physical abuse of women
and children—this is keeping. At the more personal dimension of
our lives, we even keep our own lives when we subject ourselves to
harsh self-judgment and self-hatred, or perpetually carry within us
burdens of guilt or fear. In so doing we cut off our own awareness of
and openness to the Source of our lives.

Keeping, in this sense, is the opposite of love. In the biblical context,
to love means to act or think in ways that liberate self and others. The
story of the exodus of the Israelites from Egyptian slavery illustrates
this. God acts to end enslavement, and the people are free to move
toward a new life. In the gospels of the New Testament the love of God
is manifest in Jesus as he liberates people from demon possession or
illness. He teaches them that they belong only to God, not to Rome or
to the inhuman restraints of religion that has lost its way and purpose.

Working with the ancient story of Cain and Abel had made it
even clearer to me that keeping in the case of killing another person
contradicts our true humanity, as created and sustained by God, the
Source of Life. God alone is the keeper of human beings, and for us
to assume that role in the taking of life can accomplish nothing that

is good, in spite of all the rationalizations we give for it. The nature of God is nonviolence toward us, seeking only our good. Yet the decision is always ours to make, whether or not to live in harmony with the God in whose image we are created, the Power of Life that gives birth to and sustains us.

God of Peace or God of War?

When we deal with Hebrew scriptures, we soon perceive conflicting images and stories of God. There is God who is compassion, who continually seeks the healing of human life. In the story of the expulsion of Adam and Eve from the Garden of Eden, it is not God who rejects humans, but the other way around. In a tender and profound conclusion to the story, even though the human beings have become estranged through their own doing, God "covers their nakedness" by making garments out of skin for them. This is a divine act of compassion instead of punishment. The same is true for the conclusion of the Cain and Abel story, as God places the protective mark on Cain, even though he has played God and taken the life of his brother. In the story of Noah and the great flood, God regrets ever creating humanity, which filled the Earth with violence (Genesis 6:9, 13). So broken is God's heart over the pervasive violence of human beings that God brings about the great flood, destroying all but Noah and family, and representatives of the animals. A new start is embedded within the destruction of the flood. At the end of the story, God resolves never again to deal with human violence in such a way. God returns to the Divine nature, which is compassion and love for the creation.

However, one cannot avoid the biblical picture of a God who commands capital punishment in the laws given to Israel. Or the God who orders Israel to wipe out its enemies during the invasion of the land of Canaan. We can take the approach Gandhi did with the *Bhagavad Gita* and allegorize it. The central message would be to "plunge yourself into the battle but keep your heart at the lotus feet of the Lord." In Gandhi's case, this powerful image was applied to the "battle" of nonviolence. In the stories of Israel's battles in Canaan, we would emphasize the themes of complete faithfulness to God in every way and of rejecting the worship of idols. In the Exodus story, we regard Egypt as an earthly, human power structure that oppresses others, robbing them of their freedom. Egypt represents any human power structure that "keeps" other human beings. God, the Power and Energy and Source of Life itself, stands against such structures. They have no future and will eventually collapse and die because they cut themselves off from the nature and essence of life.

In the end, there are parts of scripture we must speak against. In this case, we say that the idea of a God who demands the killing of others is an aberration within the whole of scripture. Such a notion is completely contradictory to the message of the Cain and Abel story, and of the first creation story of Genesis 1 in which men and women are together created in and share God's very image. To kill one another is to reject and deny that image. It is an assault upon God. This becomes even clearer as the story of Israel's social and moral life continues beyond the period of the conquest of the land.

Israel's life becomes settled under the monarchy and temple religion is established by Solomon's erecting of the great Jerusalem temple. The struggle changes, from that of the conquest of the land in the outward battles against the resident peoples of Canaan and their religions to the inward battles Israel must wage within herself. The cult of the temple arises and worship in the temple threatens the challenges of Israel's living faithfully in her relationship with God. Faithfulness must be shown in the people's manifesting the reign of God in their personal and national life. Israel's spiritual and communal life must reflect God's love, compassion, peace and justice. The leadership of the people, through the kings and the ever-increasing role of the prophets, must lead in this regard.

Leading up to the eventual collapse of Israel's moral life and the conquest of Israel by the forces of Babylon, the great prophets of Israel assume the role of being a moral compass. They rail against the focus on temple worship to the neglect of social and personal moral life. As the Prophet Jeremiah puts it, the people cry, "Temple of the Lord, temple of the Lord," as though right worship is more important than right living. Social injustice in the form of greed, the robbing of people by corrupt economic practices, reliance upon military strength, and general cultural malaise lead up to the events that will spell the end of the people's relationship with God and the exile of the people and their kings to Babylon. As the Prophet Hosea puts it (10:13-14), the nation has trusted in its own power and the multitude of its warriors, until trust in God alone has vanished from its life. Israel must now learn the harsh lessons of war, and of exile from God and from the land.

It is here, in the ash heap of the fall of Jerusalem and the exile, that a new vision arises. The Prophet Isaiah gives it voice:

> God shall judge between many peoples,
> and shall arbitrate between strong nations far away;
> they shall beat their swords into plowshares,
> and their spears into pruning hooks;
> nation shall not lift up sword against nation,
> neither shall they learn war any more ... .

(Isaiah 2:4)

Here is the vision of universal peace and nonviolence, arising from the mouths of the prophets, to be lived out, beginning in Israel's own life in the post-exile world. It is here that there is a return to the heart of scripture's most mature understanding of God. God is the God of nonviolent love and justice, who is to be served first of all by those who feel God's claim upon their lives. This universal vision of God's realm on Earth is to be manifested in the life of a faithful people, individually and collectively. God is no longer understood as tribal, but a global and universal God seeking the faithfulness of all nations, bestowing blessing on all who seek and live the life of God's peaceable realm. Such universal peace cannot be won through military might but only right, just, and peaceable dealings with one another as persons and as societies.

When it comes to how we live our lives and the decisions we make, if we are to do so upon the basis of our understanding of and faith in God, we must make decisions about scripture. What is the core, essential message of scripture about the nature of God and about created human nature? The nature of God is love and we are created out of that love and for that love. This cannot include a God who, at the same time, is the keeper of every human being and who also commands us to kill others for reasons of retribution, or religious or national self-interest. A choice must be made, one upon which we can base our lives. For me, the most compelling theological and spiritual vision of God was that which emerged in the time of the exile and the ministry of the great prophets of Israel. They lifted up and gave voice to a vision of God's identity and will, calling forth the best of who we are as human beings. We are created to be, and are to become again, people who live by compassion, generosity, just and peaceable relationships in the personal and social realm. This is the only way that our life can find ultimate sustenance and fruitful continuation.

4

Kill or Murder?

In Las Vegas, a man fired assault weapons from his hotel room window into a crowd of concert-goers in Las Vegas, one of the latest in the ongoing mass murders in our weapons-flooded country. I had been watching enough episodes of the PBS film *The Vietnam War* to be reminded of the massive disregard for life shown in the conduct of that war—the saturation bombings of North Vietnam and Cambodia, as well as inside South Vietnam, along with the extensive use of Agent Orange and napalm on civilian populations. That week the ecumenical Christian lectionary had dealt up the Ten Commandments portion of the Book of Exodus, chapter 20. As a conscientious objector, I have had a consistent interest in exploring the scriptures on the subject of killing. My recent sense of urgency about it had been fueled not only by this latest mass killing, but also the unabated police killings of unarmed black men and boys. Added to that were the intentionally veiled killings carried out regularly by our military in numerous countries, deaths we neither see nor seem to care about. And now we have a president who is both narcissistic and ignorant of the job to which he was elected, who carefreely and carelessly rants about a military confrontation with North Korea, inviting nuclear war. So, I was thinking again how it is that we have this commandment against killing, which Jesus intensified and made absolute in his teachings, and yet we keep on killing as though it is "just the way things are."

"You shall not kill," says Exodus 20:13. You can find the Sixth Commandment translated either, "You shall not kill" or, "You shall not murder." It is a morally convenient option. The Hebrew verb *rasah* allows for either. Yet, it leans toward "murder." This allows us to make a distinction between "legitimate" *killing* of your enemy or a criminal and "illegitimate" *murdering* of an innocent person. Anyone having a measure of familiarity with the Hebrew scriptures will see these two options clearly played out. A good number of laws and commandments have the death penalty attached. The stories of Israel's conquest of the land of Canaan are filled with the massacre of whole peoples and the confiscation of their belongings, all with divine sanction. So, it is within a biblical view to say that we may not murder innocent people, but we are free to kill those we designate as our enemies and who run afoul of our capital offense laws.

This has never satisfied me, and it does not do so now. I find tension within scripture itself on this business of killing and murdering. The story of Cain's killing of his brother returns quickly to my mind. Given that our own blood and that of others belong only to God, the motivation or rationale for taking another person's life does not matter. To shed the blood of another, for whatever reason, is to assume the role of God. Cain played God by taking the life of his brother. He "kept" his brother in the ultimate sense. Call it killing or murder, the reality is the same.

The Cain and Abel story goes to a moral place deeper than the commandment. Or, one could say that the truth of that story underlies the commandment. It expresses something about the nature of reality. It tells us that each and every human being belongs to God. Each human being has a unique and inviolable relationship to the Source and Power of Life. When we take the life of another, we are playing God. Yes, Cain murdered his brother in a fit of jealous rage. However, God puts a mark on Cain so that no other human being might take his life and thus continue the cycle of violence. Even the murderer Cain belongs to God. Right there is a pretty good case for condemning capital punishment, or any kind of retributive killing. This is a very old story in Israel's history, older than the stories of Moses. To me, it not only predates the Sixth Commandment, but places it within a more profound context. Killing and murder are essentially the same thing—human beings playing God with one another's lives.

So, is it killing? Or is it murder? The answer is yes. Killing is murder and murder is killing. Whether we do it wearing a uniform or not. Whether we use a gun or an unjust law. Whether we do it with our own hands or with a computer program guiding a rocket-equipped drone. I believe the antidote lies with each of us deciding whether or not we will continue to be part of the violence, the killing. The decisions we make about how we are going to stop contributing to the violence. The examining of our own thoughts or actions that contribute to and justify the killing. The guns we continue to purchase and brandish. The companies we work for and how they contribute to killing. Where we invest or spend our money. Our decisions whether or not to participate in the military. The ways we continue to keep silent.

The cycle of killing is broken whenever we choose no longer to be part of it or contribute to it. It must happen at many levels in our society, but it begins with how we conduct our own lives, the decisions we make, how we use the resources we have, material and spiritual, to nurture nonviolence. There came a point in my own life where it was clear that until we recognize that killing and murder are the same thing, we as a human family will not have the moral or spiritual resolve to end the violence of war that seems to thrive in our society.

5

Alternative Service

I don't remember how I first discovered the resources and process for registering as a conscientious objector. No one in the church ever talked with me about the decision whether or not to participate in the military as a moral decision, relative to Jesus' core teachings on nonviolence and love of enemies. At the time I began my search for a way to go, I did come across what I needed through the National Inter-religious Service Board for Conscientious Objectors (NISBCO), an information clearinghouse and support for COs. I obtained the proper forms from the Selective Service and began to put together my case. In the meantime, the draft instituted a lottery system in response to increasing and justified charges that military service had become a matter of the privileged and wealthy avoiding conscription, while the poor and otherwise not privileged were fodder for the war.

The lottery was based on birth dates concealed in blue plastic capsules, drawn from a turning cage on December 1, 1969. Some of us were gathered at my apartment to watch the televised event. As the agonizing process began, I went to the kitchen to get something to eat and unknowingly missed the calling of my number. For some reason, the others had missed it, as well. As the drawing continued, I felt increasing relief with the opening of each capsule and the reading of dates that were not mine. There came a pause in the drawing to recap the dates and numbers up to that point. And there it was—December 29, number 016! Suddenly everything became very real and focused. It was time to get serious and complete my application.

The Rev. Herbert "Herb" R. Moore was minister and friend to both Kaye and me during our college years and a family friend since I was a youngster. He agreed to be my clergy advocate for my appearances before the local draft board. I was fortunate in my application, for I could call upon a strong and evident religious upbringing, even though it was not in one of the historic "peace" churches, such as the Quakers or Mennonites. The Christian Church (Disciples of Christ) had a recorded history of support both for those who conscientiously participated in the military and those who opposed it. Another advantage was that Herb had appeared before this board twice before, with the only two other Vietnam-era COs, to my knowledge, to come out of Lynchburg, Virginia.

My objection was completely on religious grounds. I was asking for the classification I-O, which meant I was opposed to serving in the military. Those who chose to be non-combatant COs were classified I-A-O. A change was made in 1970 to the Selective Service guidelines for conscientious objectors that allowed objection on philosophical, or other-than-religious, grounds. I learned, however, that the change and its implementation were slow to take effect with the local boards. These boards were composed of local people from all sorts of backgrounds, charged with making estimations of the authenticity or sincerity of young peoples' beliefs. My impression was that it was rather a cloudy, if not messy, situation that put the lives and fates of young men in the hands of people not well equipped to make such judgments. At one of my appearances before the board, I waited in the hallway outside the meeting room for my turn. The door had been left slightly ajar, and I could hear the comments of board members after the young man who had been ahead of me left the building. One comment is emblazoned on my memory: "He's just afraid to die." Thus was decided the sincerity and fate of a young man whose application, apparently on the newly expanded grounds, was, I sensed, about to be rejected. By this time, I knew that my case was strong and would be approved. I would move on with my life, in a way consistent with my innermost beliefs. What would happen to that young man, who I felt to be a brother in conscience? All of this made me feel sick.

My application was approved in the early spring of 1970. Kaye and I were newly married, and now faced the task of finding a placement for my two years of civilian alternative service. Here was more confusion. We mistakenly understood that the draft board would help me find a placement. The business was finally cleared up. I had to find it on my own and present it to the board for approval. The other two Lynchburg COs had both worked at Boston Children's Hospital/Medical Center. We learned that Children's Hospital had been quite receptive to COs. Kaye's roommate and close friend in college was from Cape Cod. So, why not Boston? After graduation, we took a whirlwind trip to Massachusetts. I secured a job at the hospital and we found a one-bedroom apartment for $125 a month, a couple of blocks from Cleveland Circle and the transit for a quick ride to and from work. At the end of June 1970, our maroon Volkswagen van loaded with our sparse possessions, we were on our way.

At first, the only job offered to me at the hospital was in the shipping and receiving department. After a few months, I was able to transfer to nursing, where I had wanted to be in the first place. I then worked as a nurse's assistant on the cardiac medical and surgical division. What the direction and purpose of my life would be after those two years, I had only a vague idea. The thought of seminary was still lurking around, yet the church and "religious life" held little appeal at the time. My work as part of the nursing staff and with our young patients furnished me all the meaning and purpose I could ask for, or handle. As daily reports came from Vietnam of death, often of children, I felt grounded in the work of helping children face the physical and emotional challenges of their young lives in a hospital setting. Yet, that fact also held a painfully disconcerting contradiction. Here I was trying to help save children's lives while at the same time, half a world away, my country's military was taking the lives of others' children. Those two years probably were the most intense, focused and challenging of my life. In the end, I did enter seminary, yet often referred to the Boston years and the hospital work as my "real" spiritual, as well as theological, education and training.

As I look back over the years, through which runs the thread of coming to choose nonviolence and non-participation in the military, I have a simple and clear memory of one of the seeds of it all. Yes, it was within my upbringing in the church. For one week each summer I attended church youth camp in a beautiful Virginia mountain conference center called Craig Springs. The original name was Craig Healing Springs, for it had been built as a resort around one of the many mineral springs along the Virginia-West Virginia border. I have great appreciation of those days and of the experiences provided me and many other young people. I remember that there was very little, if any, spiritual or theological emphasis on our "original sinfulness." The weeks' themes were consistently about God's love for us and the world, God's presence in the creation, and Jesus' call to follow him in the life shaped by love, forgiveness and compassion. We talked about helping those in need, enjoying and cherishing the creation, and being peacemakers. I do not remember that the subject of military service was ever brought up as a point of discussion in our small groups. Yet, what it meant to follow Jesus was the consistent focus.

In the evenings, we would gather around a campfire, singing songs of spiritual uplift and challenge regarding the life of being Jesus' followers. The youthful, heartfelt tones of our voices would rise up into the night sky, along with the plumes of smoke and sparks from the bonfire. One of the new songs making the rounds in those years was called "Let There Be Peace on Earth." I never found it very easy or musically pleasant to sing, yet it carried the right message. I realize now, all these years later, that when we came to the last words, the musical line of which soared upward like the flames of our campfire, I had taken them with more seriousness than was apparent at the time. The words would have something to do with why I became a conscientious objector. "Let there be peace on earth … and *let it begin with me.*" And just as peace had to begin with me and the decisions I made, so did violence and war have to end with me.

6

Jesus and Nonviolence

It was a Sunday morning, sometime during Eastertide or after Pentecost. The gospel text for the day was drawn from the Gospel of Matthew, particular verses from chapter 5 of Jesus' Sermon on the Mount. Jesus' words are full of blessing for those striving for humility, peace and what he called purity of heart. Poverty, too, both spiritual and, in Luke's version (chapter 6), material. The call to nonviolence, love of one's enemy, and non-retaliation sound throughout these teachings. My sermon centered on Jesus' call to this kind of life, a life he fully believed we are capable of living. It is the life of those who are the "light of the world" and "salt of the earth," said Jesus. We are seen by Jesus, not as woe-begotten sinners, but as those created by God for the life of love, compassion, just and right relationships, and peace among ourselves and all people.

After the service, I took my usual place at the door, greeting people as they departed for their meals at home or in a restaurant. I discovered through the years that these minutes spent with people as they exited the sanctuary were rather precious. Yes, often the words were superficial. "Nice day, Reverend." "Good to see you, David." Or, a simple "Thank you." Sometimes, however, there were more significant moments. A private word that indicated someone needed to talk or needed help of some other kind. Then there were those who wanted to talk with me more deeply about something I said. And sometimes one who would take exception to the sermon or some portion of it.

On this Sunday, one of the members definitely had something on her mind. I knew her to be very devout, stemming from a kind of "salvation experience." This was during the early heydays of the now-called "evangelical" church movement. The centerpiece was coming to an experience of God's saving love in and through Jesus. This kind of religious experience was not unfamiliar to me. I grew up with some of it, attending revivals held in town by the ministerial association. My father always took part in these, but I never felt his heart was in it. He had a more studied, thoughtful, even-tempered approach to things. The language "washed in his blood," "saved by his cross," and the ever-pressing question, "Have you been saved?" was somewhat present throughout my childhood and youth. When I became a pastor, I encountered some of it wherever I roamed.

My congregant questioned my putting too much emphasis on "good works," that is, obeying Jesus' teachings. I tried to respond that Jesus probably meant what he said and meant for us to try our best to live according to what he taught. "Oh," but she retorted crisply, "that was *before* the cross and resurrection!" I didn't know what to say, for I had no clue what she was getting at. Others were waiting to speak to me and get out the door, so I thanked her and bid her a good day.

Upon reflection, I realized that what this person had done was make an incision between Jesus' life and teachings, and the crucifixion and resurrection. The teachings were rendered as relative in importance. The cross and resurrection formed a "saving event" in which one was to "believe" in order to be saved. The important thing about Jesus, then, was not what he taught or the life he lived. It was not about the importance of Jesus' call to discipleship or following the pattern of his life. Of paramount significance was the death and resurrection event as Jesus' atonement for our sinfulness. If we believe in that through a kind of emotional/spiritual experience, then we are saved and are assured of a place in heaven. How one actually lives becomes a matter of secondary importance. Too, there need be no major change in values and loyalties. For instance, one can keep the attachment to nationalism and militarism with no fear of moral conflict with being a Christian.

There are some portions of the New Testament that furnish language friendly to such a view. However, there is no justification for making how one lives of lesser value than the paramount spiritual event of "being saved." Even the apostle Paul, whose letters speak of the redemptive power of Jesus' death and resurrection, clearly and strongly thinks that being a believer in Jesus Christ means living in completely new ways, ways that are consistent with the love, compassion and justice of God. Otherwise he would not have written so many letters to the churches of his day concerning the life they were to live as Jesus' followers, both within their own fellowships and the world around them.

There is nothing in the four gospels to indicate that Jesus did not mean for us to take his teachings seriously, incorporating them in our own lives. There is nothing to suggest that Jesus thought people were somehow incapacitated by "original sin" and could not live exactly as he taught. This in itself indicates that the path to salvation— wholeness, healing, fullness of life—is found precisely in following Jesus' teachings, living them out in our own lives to the best of our ability and in the context of our present lives and life around us. Jesus said that we are the light of the world and the salt of the Earth, that we should let our lights shine forth. The light is the very life of God in us and it strives to be expressed in the ways we live and the decisions we make. Let's now take a look at Jesus' central teachings on nonviolence, and then move on to some of his teachings that have been misconstrued to present Jesus as embracing the necessity of violence.

Blessed are the peacemakers for they shall be called children of God (Matthew 5:9). The word translated "blessed" can more fully mean fortunate or happy, but in the profoundest sense of those words. If one lives out of this or the other teachings in this first section of the Sermon on the Mount, one discovers, in an unfolding way, that here is the life for which we are created. This kind of happiness has to do with living out of our truest nature as human beings.

The Greek word used for peacemakers (*eirenopoioi*) is derived from the word peace (*eirenei*). To make peace, in this sense, means to be actively living and working for peace in one's life and relationships. The word peace itself carries the meaning of harmony. To be a peacemaker, then, is to live in such a way that we are in harmony with others, are concerned for and work toward harmonious relationships in and with the world around oneself. Peacemaking is not something we do "on the side" but is at the core of our being and the heart of our interactions with others. It also has to do with how we see and engage the world in which we live.

It is this kind of life that Jesus calls blessed or completely happy. But Jesus goes further than this. Those who endeavor in this way of living are not only living out of their truest nature as human beings but also, because of this, are seen by others as "children of God." The phrase means literally those who belong to God or are begotten by God. Others will call them God's children because they are recognized as such in the peacemaking life that they live. It is important to see two things going on here. The first is that those who are peacemakers are so not in order to be seen as holy or moral, but to live out of their true humanity. The result is their own fullest happiness. Secondly, others will recognize them as children of God, seeing in them not just those doing good works but who belong to God.

Do not kill (Matthew 5:21-26). Jesus gives a rather stern warning about what he is teaching. He is not simply passing on the "law or the prophets." Neither is he doing away with what went before him. He is "fulfilling" it (Matthew 5:17). In other words, he is going even further with his teachings. He is calling for a fulfilling of the law, of those words from God that, if abided by, bring harmony and order to our lives. To fulfill means to complete or bring to full maturity. It is also going to the deepest root of what the law is meant to do, that is, lead us to living out of our created humanity.

So, Jesus says that not only is killing another human prohibited, but also anger toward another person. Anger means animosity toward another, whether it is one's spouse or friend, or a faraway individual or nation that is designated as one's enemy. The verb *phoneuo* is frequently translated as murder, when it can mean either murder or kill. Here again, we see that there is much that depends upon the view of the translator. The word murder implies an unwarranted taking of life. To kill can mean a justified taking of life, as in self-defense or in war. There is no inherent meaning in the Greek verb to support making that kind of distinction. The meaning is simply the taking of the life of another. "Keeping" one's brother or sister in the ultimate sense. Playing God.

It is not only about the action, however, but the root of the action. And Jesus places that emphasis directly on anger. Here the word means not just being angry, a passing flare-up of emotion. It means being furious with another, "so mad I can kill!" It also means retributive anger that seeks to take something back from the one who is perceived as a transgressor. From this point, Jesus speaks of the conciliatory work necessary to deal with anger when it arises. We all experience angry emotions. What concerns Jesus is what we do with them. So, Jesus gives a primary example. If I am going to make an offering to God at the temple but remember that someone "has something against" me, then I first have to go and make peace, restore harmony, with that person. It is interesting and intensifying of this teaching that Jesus puts the burden on me and not the other person! I am to be so interested in being a peacemaker in the case of killing and anger that I am engaged in dealing with myself, my own anger or sense of being wronged, and NOT the other person's liability toward me. This is not blaming oneself but letting go of one's ego so that peacefulness can replace an atmosphere or relationship of violence. It is defusing the bomb in one's own heart and mind, as well as in relationships. It means dropping from my own inner life the whole enterprise of creating and naming others as enemies or those who deserve my anger or violence. Instead, I live in full awareness that this other person is my sister or brother in God's love (Matthew 5:24).

Loving one's enemies, or loving with the love of God (Matthew 5:43-48). Another of Jesus' core teachings on nonviolent living is loving one's enemies. "You have heard that it was said, 'You shall love your neighbor and hate your enemy.' But I say to you, Love your enemies and pray for those who persecute you, so that you may be children of your Father in heaven." Jesus refers to how things have been, the laws and traditions of the past. He has come to fulfill or go to the heart of the law (Matthew 5:17). Here we have a radical expansion of the law of love, beyond those we consider neighbor. In the Greek, "neighbor" means the one who is near. Near can indicate one who is nearby in a spatial sense—my neighborhood, my town or city, my religious community with whom I worship. Or neighbor also can mean the one who is near in the sense of being like me with respect to religion, ethnicity, nationality, or shared sentiments and viewpoints.

Hebrew scripture clearly says we are to love the neighbor: "You shall not take vengeance or bear a grudge against any of your people, but you shall love your neighbor as yourself: I am the Lord" (Leviticus 19:18). In this text, the neighbor is obviously "your [own] people." Jesus considers the greatest of the commandments to be love of God and of the neighbor as oneself (Mark 12:28-32; also found in the Gospels of Luke and Matthew). The instruction to hate one's enemies is nowhere to be found in scripture. However, the Psalms contain numerous expressions of hating and punishing one's enemies or those who are considered unrighteous. In Psalm 18: "I pursued my enemies and overtook them … I struck them down, so that they were not able to rise." Or Psalm 139: "O that you would kill the wicked, O God, and that the bloodthirsty would depart from me … Do I not hate those who hate you, O Lord … I hate them with perfect hatred; I count them my enemies." Jesus may be referring to the quasi-religious, cultural approval of hating those who are not considered one's neighbor. If my neighbors are my fellow Christians, then I am free to bear hostility toward non-Christians. If my neighbors are those of my own race, then I am free to act and think in racist ways toward others.

It is significant, then, if not shocking, that Jesus extends the responsibility to love beyond the neighbor, to the near one, to the enemy, the "far" one. The word for love is *agape*, meaning the kind of love that is like God's love. It is a lovingkindness that regards the other person as a child of God, just as I am. Even the enemy. Even the one who "persecutes" me. The word used here literally means the one who comes after me, who pursues me. In both instances, we are to love with the love of God. Put another way, we are to extend toward others, whether neighbor, enemy or pursuer, the love with which we are loved. The First Letter of John puts it succinctly: "Beloved, since God loved us so much, we also ought to love one another (4:11)." This is also made clear when Jesus says that we are to love our enemies and pray for those who persecute us so that we "may be children of your Father in heaven." As human beings, our truest nature is to live in a way that manifests the Love that is the Source of Life, that is at the heart of the universe, which we call God. It is a life that unwaveringly and stalwartly regards all human beings as brothers and sisters. Left to culturally formed ways of loving, we cannot do it. Living and loving by drawing upon the supreme love that comes from God, however, it is possible. Jesus seems to have fully believed that we are, by our created nature, capable of living the way he taught.

What does it mean to love both neighbor and enemy in this way? What does such lovingkindness, or loving regard for others, look like? Being children of this love, this God, means perceiving and acting toward others with equity or impartiality. A Buddhist teaching says that the rose doesn't give its fragrance to some but not to others. That is the same impartiality we are to show our fellow human beings. In Jesus' case, he refers to God who makes the sun rise on both the evil and the good, and causes the rain to fall on the righteous and unrighteous. The way of God's love, then, is just like the ways of the Earth and the universe: it is given to all human beings, regardless of how they act, who they are, or what they believe. And it is this love with which Jesus commands us to love. This kind of loving, this way of living, reveals that we are children of God, that we are true human beings in the way we are created to be.

Jesus goes on to say that if we love only those who love us, who are like us, what reward do we have? Even tax collectors do that. These were Jews who collaborated with the Roman tax system, thus were considered sinners. Even Gentiles, disdained as nonbelievers in Jesus' day, greet only their brothers and sisters. Jesus' calls us beyond such limited love to a kind of loving that fulfills our true, given nature. "Be perfect, therefore, as your heavenly Father is perfect." The word for perfect also means to be fulfilled or complete. The kind of impartial, universal love Jesus taught resonates with and completes, or fulfills, our true humanity.

This teaching on love that includes the enemy runs counter to our culture. In our current political climate, there is a strong movement toward division into those who are my political "neighbors" and those who are my political "enemies." We have lost the capacity or will to disagree with others and at the same time treat them with respect as fellow human beings, then to work together for the common good. Our country is carrying on wars in several other countries, against those regarded as our enemies. The enemy is designated not only ISIS or the Taliban, but also any political movement that we consider not in our country's interest. Therefore, we not only have direct and open military invasions, such as in Afghanistan or Iraq, but also the "regime change" foreign policy of covertly involving ourselves in the affairs of other countries. In all cases, we are surrounded by the rhetoric of having and hating enemies. Young people who enlist in the military go through intense training to regard the enemy as the "other" and to objectify the enemy sufficiently to kill. The teachings of Jesus do not allow such objectifying and labeling, much less the accompanying hate or killing. Jesus' teaching on love of the enemy calls us to the fullness of who we are as children of God through a kind of love that cannot disregard others' kindred humanity.

7

Jesus *and* Violence

Attempts always have been made to construct a picture of Jesus that makes room for violence and killing. We have a cultural commitment to the necessity, in certain circumstances, of harming or taking the life of other human beings. The dominant form of this commitment is, of course, the military as the nation's primary means of confronting and eliminating those defined as our enemies, who stand in the way of our "national interests."

For those in churches, whether by choice or cultural habit, the dilemma lies in encountering the scriptural picture of Jesus and his collected teachings, as remembered and valued by the early religious communities of his followers. At the core of Jesus' teachings are those explicitly condemning killing, calling for love of enemies, and rejecting retributive action of any kind. Jesus' life as portrayed in the gospels manifests these moral qualities to a degree that leaves no room for violence in the lives of those who choose to follow him, then or now.

Still, the effort is made to include violence in the Christian life. So-called "evangelical" churches in the U.S. make no bones about a Jesus who condones the legitimized killing of war, that is, our own wars. The military is celebrated and blessed without the slightest theological or moral flinching. In Lynchburg, Virginia, where we lived for many years, the late Jerry Falwell Sr.'s church, in conjunction with his Liberty University, holds an annual "Celebrate America" day. It is no surprise that the dominant themes of the festival are national zeal and military pride. Nowhere is there a glimpse of the Jesus of the Christian scriptures. However, the uncritical coexistence of espoused Christian faith and militant nationalism, which legitimizes killing in the name of the state, is found in mainline churches, as well, Protestant and Catholic. It simply has become part of the fabric of Christianity in this country. One need only raise the question of the teachings of Jesus on nonviolence, as well as the pattern of his life, to stir up a hornets' nest.

As a pastor and preacher, who is also a conscientious objector, I have ventured, unknowingly or intentionally, into matters of the military, war and the life of following Jesus. A member of the small rural congregation I served while a seminary student was a farmer and a veteran of World War II. It was from him I learned that, in most cases, those who have experienced the realities of the killing inherent to military service are least eager to talk about them. In such men I have found a Christian faith that is deeply humble, without arrogance or even the kind of self-assuredness that often passes as religious belief. On the other hand, there have been those, a few of whom served in the military, but, oddly, not most, who have taken quick offense whenever I have taught or preached concerning Jesus and violence. Some of these have given the most emotional defense of the use of violence, straining to find something in Jesus' life and teachings that gives support to their views. I learned through the years that the degree of emotional heat was generated by awareness, at a deep level, that there is, after all, no foundation in Jesus for his followers to justify violence, even that of national or self-defense.

I was taken to task on one occasion following something I said in a sermon about the violent past, as well as present, of our country. The words were in response to one of the mass shootings that have become horribly routine in our country. As followers of Jesus, I said, we must confront our racist and violent history if we are to shape a different present and future. Conjointly, I questioned why a Christian would feel justified in owning a gun. Following worship, I was accosted by a very angry man who had been worshipping with our community. He was a devout gun owner, though not a veteran. He saw himself as a Christian. And yet, there was in him this deep-seated commitment to a rightful place for violence that had been pricked by both my words and my having been a conscientious objector. This was neither a unique nor isolated experience in my years as a pastor. In some cases, no attempt was made to seek biblical or theological support. In others, there was a predictable collection of Jesus' teachings and stories about Jesus that were called as witnesses for a violence-embracing Christian life and faith. All were based upon misunderstandings and misinterpretations of the texts themselves. Given the clarity and centrality of Jesus' explicit teachings against killing and violence, even the most tentatively plausible case could not be maintained. Let's visit each of these briefly, yet sufficiently to show that even these teachings and stories are themselves part of Jesus' essential teachings about the necessity of nonviolence for a life that is truly human as we are created to be human.

I came to bring a sword (Matthew 10:34). Probably the most frequently presented of Jesus' teachings by those who want to maintain both their Christian identity and the necessity of violence is found in Jesus' words, "Do not think that I have come to bring peace on the earth; I have not come to bring peace, but a sword" (Matthew 10:34). The sword, of course, is taken literally by those who want to see it so. This ignores the use of symbolic words in the Bible, words that point to something other than their face value. If we are going to read sacred religious texts in any tradition, we must understand and recognize the employing of symbolism. The realities to which some words direct us lie beyond the limits of human expression, and yet only words can lead us there. To take them literally, or on their face value, is to miss the whole meaning of what is being expressed.

In this case, Jesus is talking about the seriousness of what it means to follow him in terms of attachments. Deciding to follow the way he is teaching and leading means detachment from other loyalties and commitments. It is helpful to see this played out in a different way in Luke 12:49-53. There Jesus uses the symbolic word "fire" to make the same point. When he asks if his disciples think that he has come to bring peace to the Earth, he clarifies it. No, not peace but division. Jesus is speaking of the "last times" when everything will be judged. The things that he has been teaching and showing have to do with the ultimate outcome of life, so that "from now on" there will be the division he indicates by the use of the word "sword" in Matthew 10. Jesus' work and calling are to bring people to a point of decision about their lives in relation to God. The ultimate value in our lives is touched as we live from our relationship to the Power and Presence that undergirds and infuses all of life, which we call God. Only that kind of fundamental decision, or sword, can relieve us from lesser values that tend to obscure and keep us from what ultimately matters. The way of Jesus is that of loving God with our whole being—body, mind, spirit, strength. And then loving others as we love ourselves. Only attachment to this way of living can bring fullness of life to us and our relationships with the world around us. The completeness of love that flows from first loving God comes only as we let go of impediments and attachments. The meaning of idolatry is substituting lesser loves for the supreme love, the love of God. The sword Jesus meant is that which cuts the lesser ties so that the greater tie, or faithfulness, can be fulfilled. Hate. Fear. Worry. Material wealth. Ego-centered living. One's nation or ethnicity. Religion that forgets its essential purpose. Yes, even one's family. These things can get in the way of the most important thing—faithfulness to God.

Such decisions can and almost certainly will bring us into conflict with those things and people which lay claim to our loyalties. In Jesus' teaching about the sword, he is speaking primarily of human relationships that take on the nature of attachments. Even attachments to family can stand in the way of our living primarily out of our relationship with God. Many conflicts in families occur at times when children begin choosing values that differ from their parents', or when a spouse begins to change in terms of their choices about life's meaning or purpose. We get used to and want our loved one to remain as we have known them; when they begin to change, to choose a different way, we feel abandoned, even rejected. Even as I write this, high school students in Florida, many of their friends murdered and wounded by an assault gun-wielding young man, are choosing to confront the gun culture of this country and those who continue to flood our nation with weapons. In many cases, they may be choosing against the values of their families, their parents. For certain, they are using the sword of which Jesus speaks, cutting ties with adults who want things to remain the same.

The situation is frequently the same with those who choose against participation in war. For them, Jesus' sword of division cuts the tie between themselves and the war-making culture in which they live. Seeking to establish themselves in true peacefulness, they end up "at war," or in conflict, with families, friends, teachers, even their own religious communities. Taking to heart the clear teachings of Jesus about nonviolence and peacemaking, they may find themselves in tension with those around them. Yet, they most certainly will find a new "family" of all who have made similar decisions in their own lives. Out of such cutting of the ties with war come new alliances with those who have given themselves unyieldingly to the ways of peace and peacemaking. And in other cases, there will be parents, friends, teachers, spiritual leaders who will perceive exactly what they are doing, will know that moral deepening and maturity come at the cost of such decisions, and will offer their approval, support, and blessing.

A whip of cords/Jesus cleanses the temple. The story of Jesus "cleansing of the temple" is one frequently used by those who insist on finding violence legitimated in Jesus' teachings and life. The story is found in all four gospels. Matthew 21:12-22, Mark 11:15-19 and Luke 19:45-48 place the story at the end of Jesus' ministry, when he has entered Jerusalem for the final confrontation with religious and political authorities. John 2:13-22 puts the event at the very beginning of Jesus' ministry, as though he is making a statement right off the bat concerning the pollution of religion by power and money interests. Only here do we find Jesus using a "whip of cords (or rope)." The verse in which this is found is curious. Jesus uses the whip to drive "all of them out of the temple." However, this "all" is qualified in the last part of the sentence to mean "both the sheep and the cattle." Evidently Jesus does not use the whip on people. Whether or not he actually hit the animals is not made clear either. In Matthew and Mark, Jesus overturns the tables used by the money changers and sellers, which is, at worst, an offense against property. Luke says only that Jesus enters the temple and starts driving out the merchants. Adding the versions together, we find that the only common denominator is Jesus' action of driving from the temple those who would use it as a site for making profits.

It is right to say that the story shows that Jesus had the capacity for what we call "righteous anger." That is, when he saw human injustice or a cheapening of the essential nature of religion, his anger was aroused. He responded in word and action. However, it is an unjustifiable jump from a "whip of cords" to any kind of weapon used to threaten or take the life of human beings. It is equally unacceptable to make Jesus' righteous anger into an excuse for our own hatred of others or our objectification of them to the point of killing them.

The point of the story is that the place for the worship of God has become a marketplace. Religion has become a moneymaking enterprise. The true purpose of religion, to awaken people to God and their relationship with and life in God, has been subsumed by greed and the power that comes with society's version of success. Jesus' "zeal for the house of God" (John 2:17) has the same function and meaning as the "sword of division" of which Jesus speaks in Matthew 10. His concern is for single-minded, single-hearted devotion to and love of God, and the life of faithfulness that flows from that devotion, that love. He is opposed to a mingling of religion and culture to the detriment of religion's true nature and purpose.

This story speaks directly to the predicament of religion today. The church has bought into and sells the values of our culture when it comes to nationalism and militarism. It is preoccupied with its own perpetuation and growth in terms of money and membership, thus bartering away its central reason for being. Instead of calling and challenging people to live their lives in relation to God, the church has become a commercial operation, continually seeking new enticements to "get people into church." American nationalism and militarism are made part of the church's blend of enticements. Since we are a culture that values so highly nationalistic fervor and militaristic might, the church simply adds these into the mix, without question. It is evident in something so simple, yet visible, as national flags in church sanctuaries. Military service, therefore, is the norm within the culture of the church in the U.S., whether in the garish style of evangelical churches or the softer tones of the mainline, even progressive, churches. Those who "serve their country" are favorably recognized, while those who choose against military service precisely because of their faithfulness to Jesus' teachings and life are overtly condemned, quietly shunned or ignored.

Jesus and concealed carry (Luke 22:38). One of the more interesting stories related to the issue of Jesus and violence is found toward the end of Luke's gospel. The scene is the arrest of Jesus by the temple police who are brought along by some elders and chief priests. These come armed and ready to apprehend Jesus by force if necessary. Says Jesus: "Have you come out with swords and clubs as if I were a bandit?" (Luke 22:52)

It is important to read the scene prior to the actual arrest, where Jesus talks with the disciples about being prepared. "When I sent you out without a purse, a bag, or sandals, did you lack anything?" He refers to instructions earlier in their ministry when he sent the disciples out to heal, cast out demons, and proclaim the realm of God (Luke 9:3). Now, however, Jesus says it is time to bring everything with them. Purse, bag, sandals. Even a sword! Why? Jesus' explanation is that this is to fulfill scripture, specifically, Isaiah 53:12, so that he must "be counted among the lawless." Right here, then, we see that the swords will serve a symbolic, theological purpose. For Jews to pick up swords, arming themselves, is a sign of resistance against Roman rule, of lawlessness.

The disciples then respond, "Lord, look, here are two swords." Evidently some of the disciples were armed already. Concealed carry. Jesus responds: "It is enough." His quick reply ends the whole matter of everyone having a sword. There are enough to serve the purpose, which is *not* intended violence. This becomes clear at the conclusion of the story. In Lukas 22:49-50, "those around" him, presumably the disciples, ask if it is time to strike out with the sword. Before Jesus can answer, one of them whips out a sword and slices off the ear of a slave. Immediately, Jesus puts it to an end. "No more of this!" The reply is strong and decisive. Jesus touches the man's ear and heals him. At this point, the matter is settled. The swords were to be props to fulfill the words of the prophet about the messiah, the servant of God who is to go through suffering, and not to gain victory through violence. The swords were symbolic. The healing was real. It was the latter that defined Jesus' purpose and mission, and was to be that of his followers.

Again, we see that only by lifting some of Jesus' words out of context can a case be made for weapons and violence. And once more we find an example of the use of symbolism in scriptures. The symbolism can be ignored, but only at the cost of understanding what Jesus really was about. He does not condone the use of weapons to harm and kill, even in his defense. This scene in Luke's gospel speaks eloquently against all uses of violence either to defend or to further the cause of a religion called Christianity. In this vein, we need only read the history of Spain's armed conquest of Central and South America in the 1700s and beyond. Or the rest of Europe's invasion of North America and near-extermination of Native American people and their culture. In both cases, the rallying cry was to take up both the cross *and* the sword or gun.

We may think that such a welding together of the symbol of love that suffers for the sake of others and that of violent conquest is over. Yet, behind all our wars stands a religion that lends its spiritual support, either overtly or by silent consent. Our prominent pastors bless the troops and pray for those who instigate and preside over the battles. Our sanctuaries display the national flag together with a religious flag and a cross sitting somewhere, on a communion table or above an altar. Rarely, if ever, do we hear Jesus' words to us: "No more of this!"

8

Children and Violence

What I have seen in young children has done nothing to confirm anything like "original sin" in them. I believe that the common secular version of our original sinfulness is the notion that we are born with a propensity for violence. All that I have learned from my experiences with children has convinced me that we are all born with original goodness. In Islam there is the belief that every child is born in *fitrah*, a state of original goodness and submission in relation to God. This coincides with the first creation story of Genesis 1, in which the human beings, along with the rest of the creation, are pronounced good. The spiritual/theological writer Matthew Fox makes this case persuasively and thoroughly in his book *Original Blessing* (1983). Because of many social factors—parents and other adults, television, movies, computers, cultural formation and so forth—throughout our formative years, our original goodness or *fitrah* is either reinforced and deepened, or covered over and bent toward self-centeredness, materialism, violence or any combination of these.

I vividly recall a discussion one day in a seminary class. The topic of original sin came up. One of my colleagues was swift to offer his testimony on the subject. He was convinced that we are, indeed, born sinful, a conviction that came from what he saw as the innate selfishness of small human beings. They cry when they want food or when their diaper needs changing. They cry because of all such selfish desires. Besides what I saw as wanton ignorance, I was equally appalled that no one but I offered any rebuttal to this superficial and unexamined argument. This included the silence of the professor. In my then recent experience of caring for children in a hospital setting, where needs were many and great, I had seen children cry for many reasons. Hunger. Hurt. Fear. Unnamable, for them, discomforts and needs that could be expressed only with tears. I saw nothing that came close to some kind of original blotch on young souls. Rather, what I saw in plentiful evidence was compassion, trust, and lovingkindness with which we come originally equipped.

While working at Children's Hospital in Boston, my assignments were mostly the boys, as I was the only male on the nursing staff of the cardiac medical and surgical division. As some of the toughest patients happened to be young males, the charge nurses would give them to me, often with a wry smile. I smiled back, good-naturedly charging them with female chauvinism, assuming that since I was male, I was hefty and strong—not the case in reality—and therefore most capable of wrestling with the toughest of cases.

One of my older patients was Alan, around 16 at the time. He suffered from congenital hemophilia, the bleeding disorder leaving him vulnerable to danger from the least bump and bruise. His family was on vacation at Cape Cod and Alan had an accident that quickly landed him in our hospital. While he was my patient, we had many lively conversations and I found him to be a contented, confident and affable teenager. He was learning to play the banjo, so we had much to talk about—the origin of the banjo, styles of playing, and famous banjo players, like Pete Seeger and his famous long-neck folk banjo. Everything I saw in Alan convinced me of the reality of our original goodness. I remember a conversation with Alan's father about his experience with his son. He told me that, though he and his wife deeply loved their son and tried to safeguard him, they finally realized they could not pad the whole world for him. I believe it was out of this kind of loving yet freedom-giving care that they were raising a child in ways that nourished his original goodness and strength.

In like manner, I came to know Denny, another lively and optimistic teenager. He was my assignment on several occasions. Denny, like many of our patients, suffered from congenital heart disease. Some of our young patients also came with what we called, only among ourselves, "cardiac cripple" syndrome. That is, they had been sheltered and protected by their parents to an extent that it inhibited their innate abilities, strengths and courage. This was not blaming their parents, for we knew that this kind of caring came from love. However, it was a love that smothered and shielded rather than built upon a child's inborn capacities for outgoingness and the full embracing of their lives.

Denny was no cardiac cripple. He was energetic, loved joking around, and it brightened us up whenever we heard he was to be admitted. I got to know Denny quite well over the course of his periodic hospitalizations. He was an eager student at school. There were stories of his bounding up the steps of the school, having to stop and sit on the landings to catch his breath. Denny also held down a part-time job painting sailboats.

What was different about patients like Alan and Denny? The nursing staff wanted to explore this question, for it was integral to our work and to a better understanding of our patients. So, we invited Denny's mother to come to one of our patient care rounds and talk with us. One story told it all. When Denny was about 6 or 7 years old, she said, he was out in the backyard playing. All of a sudden, he bolted toward the back fence with the clear intent of hoisting himself over it. This was an effort that could have cost him his life. His mother was in the kitchen and happened to look out the window at just that moment. Her first impulse was to rush to the door and scream at him to stop. Instead, she sat down at the table and cried. If Denny was to live a full life, short as it may be because of his heart deficiency, she would have to let him go. We were stunned! The fullness of Denny's original goodness was allowed to flourish by a caring mother who understood the risk of authentic love.

Daniel's story was different, but in a most important way, the same. He had rheumatic heart disease, a symptom of which was a puffiness that gave his 12-year-old face a cherubic appearance. During his hospital stays, which were sometimes quite lengthy, he was well and eager enough to be allowed privileges. I was given permission to "spring him from the joint" and take him on outings. The favorite destination was Fenway Park, with its famous "green monster" left-field wall. The only photo I have of myself with one of my patients is of Daniel and me on one of the baseball excursions. We were sitting together on the steps of a fountain we passed on our way to the ballpark. I had asked a passerby to do me the honor of taking our picture with my beloved Minolta rangefinder. There was Daniel, sporting his baseball cap, in a T-shirt and jeans, and me with my shoulder length hair, flowered shirt and bell-bottomed pants. I treasure that photo and the memory of that day.

In one important aspect, Daniel's story was different from the others. One day his father, a brash, angry, Boston Irish, blue-collar guy, made a rare and brief visit to his hospitalized son. What I remember most from that occasion was how this man argued with us, the nursing staff, that there was "nothing wrong with my boy." If he could not *see* the actual illness, it was not real to him. He would not accept that his son's sickness was an actual thing. Therefore, he could not accept his son. In spite of this, however, I found Daniel to be a resilient, though somewhat repressed, child.

One day we received on the division, for some reason, a neurological patient named Stephen. For the few days of his hospitalization, he was in my care. Stephen was very quiet, and yet we got to know each other pretty well. Maybe this was because I was always a quiet sort myself; we were kindred spirits. Stephen had a history of seizures. As a precaution, the head nurse taped a gauze-padded tongue depressor to his headboard. We made our own in those days. This was to be placed between Stephen's teeth should there be a seizure. Only once on my watch did Stephen have a seizure. I learned from Stephen that his mother wanted him to become a priest, applying a good deal of pressure in that direction. The day of the seizure, the first tremors began following a visit from his mother. I placed the tongue depressor in his mouth as directed, then alerted the charge nurse. I took a seat beside Stephen's bed and began to speak to him reassuringly, holding his hand. I noticed that while I was talking to him, the seizure began to subside. This suggested to me that the seizure might have been triggered by his mother's visit and something in their relationship. In other words, the convulsions at least might have an emotional as well as physiological basis. When one of the intern doctors came in for his rounds, I spoke with him about what I had observed. This brought a defensive, rather arrogant, response to the effect that I was "playing doctor" and should keep my diagnoses to myself. It was one of those moments that I regret not having enough emotional spine. I wish I had been able to rejoin something like, "Well, it seems that you are the one playing doctor instead of being a doctor who welcomes anything that might improve the care for your patients!" But I have many such rueful moments in my life, which I must continue to put aside, as I finally am learning at so late a date, to be more forthright. I realized that Stephen had some great struggles ahead of him. His mother, out of the only sort of love she was able to give, without knowing it, had damaged his original goodness by crippling him emotionally. I have thought of him many times, praying that he found the inner strength and resilience to be his true, authentic self. Perhaps a priest, after all, but by his choice and calling, not the result of his mother's pressuring.

Perhaps my greatest teacher was Ricky. He, too, was a regular on the cardiac division. Ricky was a heavyweight, quiet, resistant early teenager with Down Syndrome. He was mine to watch over on his visits. Connecting with Ricky was one of the greatest and most rewarding challenges I had in my life. My efforts to communicate and establish some kind of bond were rebuffed continually by his refusal to talk to me and his stubborn "huh-uh!" whenever I asked for his cooperation in some task, like taking his blood pressure or temperature, making his bed, or giving him a bed-bath. He sat cross-legged on his bed each morning, giving me a quiet yet guarded look whenever I entered the room. One day, however, as I was rounding his bed, he reached out and grabbed the stethoscope which I habitually stuffed in the back pocket of my dark green uniform pants. He held it behind his back, daring me to try and retrieve it, a grin on his face. We had made it, finally, Ricky and I! After that, we had many wonderful times together. The best ones were on spring days when I was able to take Ricky in a wheelchair to the hospital garden. There he delighted in everything, from a crumpled cigarette package, glinting with the sunlight as he held it close to his face, to a string bass played by a member of an Irish band that had come to entertain the children. Ricky insisted on my wheeling him so close to the instrument that he could reach out and touch where the sound was coming from.

The bond between Ricky and me was no secret. It was greatly appreciated, especially on the day Ricky was due to go to radiology. He got wind of it, got out of bed, and wedged himself under the bathroom sink. It took more time than my schedule allowed for me to coax him out of his refuge. We finally did it and were off for X-rays in the nick of time. My relationship with Ricky drew the respect of the rest of the staff. This was, after all, at the heart of our work with the children. Gaining their trust. Treating them with respect. In other words, love in action.

The day when Ricky was to undergo heart surgery, I was working the second shift. I came up in the elevator and when the doors opened, there stood Joan, the charge nurse. She had been waiting for me to tell me the news of Ricky's death in surgery. She led me to the staff's break room, spoke with me briefly of how she knew what Ricky meant to me and how sorry she was. Then she left me alone until I felt like coming on the floor. Ricky's life and death still speak to me profoundly of the original goodness with which we are born, and how that goodness survives and bears witness.

I have spent a great deal of time in the company of children, as a nursing caregiver, a teacher of music, a pastor, a father and grandfather. I have seen nothing that persuades me of an original sinfulness that bends us toward violence. I have not seen evidence of our being born with a kind of moral neutrality that can go either way. What I have witnessed is a strong and resilient bent toward kindness and love, a concoction that nourishes inner strength. When I hear someone talk about how we are born with a propensity for violence, I have to respond, "You don't spend enough time with children." It makes me wonder about such persons' own lives and how their original goodness and peaceableness might have been thwarted or otherwise harmed so that they cannot see it in themselves or others.

One of Jesus' core teachings was the place of children. They are to be at the center of our lives. They teach us what true living is about, what Jesus called the kingdom or realm of God. It is life as it is created and meant to be lived. When the disciples of Jesus were arguing over who was the greatest among them, Jesus put a child in their midst and told them that they must be able to receive, or welcome, a small child in order to welcome, or be open to, God (Mark 9:37). In other ways, Jesus taught that being close to children is necessary for understanding what it means to live as a true human being. It puts us back in touch with our own *fitrah*, our true nature. And that way of living, that true nature, does not include violence, much less killing.

9

What Belongs to God

In the Gospel of Matthew 22:15-21 there is a story of some disciples of the Pharisees and some Herodians, a royal family supportive of Rome, approaching Jesus. They want to entrap him, to expose him either as a supporter of Rome's oppressive taxation law or an opponent, perhaps even a Zealot. One way, he offends his own people. The other, he offends Rome. Jesus sees through the game and turns the tables on them. First, they try to butter him up. "Teacher, we know your sincerity, and that you teach the way of God without favoritism." Their flattering words have no effect. Jesus is consistently focused on what is true, not his own ego. There are some words of an early Buddhist teaching that describe Jesus' integrity: "As a solid rock cannot be moved by the wind, the wise are not shaken by praise or blame" (*The Dhammapada*, Buddhist). Right here we have something to think about. It has to do with our own interior work, so that we are less concerned with pleasing or impressing people, or with conforming to societal standards than with what is true and sound, the "way of God."

Let us pay attention to what Jesus does, not only what he says. Jesus' actions are as important as his words. What does Jesus do? He asks to see one of the coins used for paying the tax, a denarius. Notice that Jesus himself does not possess a coin. That's something else to think about. Jesus travels light and calls us to do the same. He teaches about the dangers of accumulating earthly treasures, and he lives what he teaches. We certainly do not travel as light as Jesus. However, he continues to show us that we can do with less material, as well as cultural, baggage. The lighter we travel, the more freely and trustfully we live. Our moral vision is also clearer. We are increasingly liberated from the values proffered by the materialist, nationalistic culture in which we live.

Jesus takes the coin and asks whose likeness is on it. The emperor's, of course. What would be on our coins? Well, maybe a buffalo, if it is a nickel we hold! Or a past president. The words "The United States of America." But also—and get this—"In God We Trust." We actually put words on our money saying that we trust in God! I don't believe there are that many of us who separate God and money, who actually trust God more than money. Our coins tell the truth: We trust money AS our god. And all that money stands for—materialism, power, accumulation of wealth at the expense of others' labor and their poverty. We idolize the wealthy and put them on our boards and into the highest offices in the land, believing that there is a real connection between wealth and wisdom. This is a good one also for religious communities to consider. How might we *say* we trust and serve God, while attaching our security to money, property and all that goes with them?

Now we can see Jesus handing the coin back. "Well, then," he says, "give to Caesar what belongs to Caesar and to God what belongs to God." And that's it. The story ends with Jesus' questioners being "amazed," more literally meaning dumbfounded. They don't know what to say. The matter is put right back to them and they cannot escape it. The whole thing has blown up in their faces. Why? Because Jesus refused to deal at the level of political maneuvering or religious posturing. All those games, all that subterfuge! His sole interest is God, that greater Reality within which we live, and the call of every human being to live faithfully, trustingly in relation to God.

So, what *is* the emperor's and what *is* God's? It is clear but at the same time weightier than we might think. Give Caesar the coin, the tax. His picture is on it. It is his. But … give to God what is God's. What belongs to God? Listen to Psalm 24: "The earth is the Lord's and everything that is in it; the world and all those who live in it." The words of that psalm speak for the whole of scripture. What belongs to God? The Earth, the creation, the universe—everything, including our own lives. Remember the story of Cain and Abel. When Cain kills his brother, Abel, his brother's blood cries out to God from the ground. The blood, the very life of Abel and all of us belongs to God alone. Jesus' blood is poured out for us. Do you know what that means? Not some bloody religious sacrifice. No. His blood is his life. It belongs to God. He lived that way and he died that way. He was killed because he lived his life as giving-God-what-is-God's. The religious and political establishment couldn't stand it. It had no hold on him. He showed us that this is how we are to live, as well. Our lives belong to God, not to the emperor, or the contemporary equivalent.

It was this story, this teaching that spoke to me so clearly about what I must do when I became a conscientious objector. The depth of its truth has unfolded increasingly throughout the years. My life, my whole being, belongs to God alone. The problem is that we continue to give to Caesar what is God's. And the emperor seldom has the same purposes as God. The emperor asks us to go along with injustice, with uploading the nation's wealth to those who are far wealthier than anyone should be. The emperor justifies robbing children of health care or equal educational opportunities. The emperor demeans those who are in need and seeking shelter, while uplifting the powerful and wealthy as moral examples. The emperor asks us to kill, to take others' blood, which belongs to God alone, for the emperor's purposes. The emperor asks us to cooperate in the destruction of the sacred creation that belongs only to God, that is entrusted to us as stewards, caretakers.

So, this little story is like dynamite. It has *dunamis*, power to blow apart our lesser loyalties and power to generate a life completely given to God, to the purposes for which we were created. Jesus says, in essence, to his questioners, "Here, take your little coin back. Give it to Caesar. But give everything else to God. Do that, and you will stop living a useless life of subterfuge and moral confusion. You will begin to live the only truly fulfilling life—a life given back to God." And, we might add, it may happen that circumstances dictate that even that little coin, the tax, will be withheld because it, too, belongs ultimately to God and God's purposes. All of life, including our own life, belongs to God, from whom it flows as a gift. Therefore, the most authentic and fulfilling way to live as human beings is to do so in ways that give our lives back to God, and to God alone. When we stop giving to the emperor what belongs to God, we will start to live in life-giving ways.

10

A CO in the Church

As I approached the end of my seminary studies, I faced a fork in the road. Down one path lay entering a doctoral program in philosophy. My sense of purpose regarding ministry within the church was shaky. The two years I had worked at Boston Children's Hospital, plus the alienation from the church I experienced as a conscientious objector, caused me to question my sense of calling to pastoral ministry. At the same time, my experience serving as a student minister in a small rural church in northern Kentucky had told me that there was, indeed, something of a call to serve within the church that had, to a great extent, nourished my spiritual well-being.

My heart simply wasn't in the prospects of a life in academia. I suspected that it would lead to an arid existence. I realized that I had a heart for ministry, a head for theology, and some life experience that made me wonder whether or not the church wanted to deal with the real world and its real problems, such as violence and war. Besides, I had no confidence that a congregation would want to hire a CO as their pastor. It was in the midst of this quandary that I received a phone call from the chair of a congregational search committee. The church was located just outside of Lexington, Kentucky, halfway between Lexington, where we lived, and my wife's hometown of

Paris. Antioch Christian Church (Disciples of Christ) was right in the middle of the lush and lovely horse farms of Fayette and Bourbon counties. The caller was telling me that the committee was interested in me precisely *because* I was a CO! The deal was sealed. I began my ministerial career with six years serving a small, progressive, rural congregation in which we could talk about things that really mattered and what the church as a community of Jesus' followers was truly about—compassion, justice, peacemaking, loving one another and the world with God's own love.

I served only four congregations from ordination to retirement. In two of them, the message I got was another story, more in tune with most of the churches in the country. In subtle or more overt ways, I was informed that it was OK that I had been a conscientious objector, but it was hoped that I would not make a "big deal" of it. Though there may have been some admiration for my decision and experience, there was far more concern that it not become an "issue" within the congregation. There were many, after all, who had served in the military and they had to be kept in mind. It is true that through the years I encountered some hostility within the church from those who had been in the military. Often, it was from those who had never seen action in war. I found that those who had experienced the reality of warfare were more inclined to show me silent, sometimes verbal, respect. In one congregation, three veterans of the Vietnam War became close friends and supporters. The overall experience, however, of serving churches as a minister who was a conscientious objector, and who felt it important to speak about Jesus' life and teachings regarding violence, was that the church simply did not talk about it. The church in our society was so thoroughly acculturated that the default position was always in favor of nationalism and militarism. There was a consistent concern that those "who served" be honored and recognized, yet no interest in the same for those who had chosen, out of their commitment as followers of Jesus and his teachings, to serve the country and world in ways other than military.

I spent the last 13 years of my professional life as minister of a small congregation that had supported me as a college student trying to find my way through the draft dilemma. The Church of the Covenant, affiliated with the United Church of Christ, in Lynchburg, Virginia, became known to me through my volunteering as a tutor to inner-city children, a ministry started out of that tiny fellowship. I frequented the Lodge of the Fisherman, a coffeehouse run by one of the church's mission groups. There I would play or listen to folk music, mingle with some of the church members and others, and talk about the war, our society, the church … things that mattered to me and others who had discovered the Lodge as a safe haven for spiritual seekers who were not at ease with the church as they had experienced it. The minister of the church was the Rev. Beverly Cosby, whose older brother Gordon and his wife, Mary, had founded a similar community, the Church of the Saviour, in Washington, D.C. Here was a Christian spiritual community which, it was evident to me, had things right. Being a Christian was about responding to Jesus' call to follow him, giving disciplined attention to what one felt was God's call in one's life, and discovering the gifts one had been given by God to use in the service of others and the world. It was a community that, through its own history, had tried to learn and live the meaning of Bonhoeffer's costly discipleship. As I was moving into the last decade or so of my ministerial life, and about to give up on further service in the traditionally structured church, I was given the opportunity to return as pastor to and member of this little band of people working with deep commitments to their faith, inwardly and outwardly.

Since retiring, my concern has grown that we as a society, and the church in particular, have not addressed, but have avoided, the question of morality and military service. We have been learning about the realities of war and its effect on participants. The term post-traumatic stress disorder (PTSD) is now familiar, clinically and in the lives of our families and friends. In recent times, the phrase "moral injury" has become increasingly familiar, recognizing that warfare puts men and women in situations in which their sense of morality is shattered by actions they have taken or have been forced to take. The killing of non-combatants—men, women and children—for instance. It is my belief that PTSD and moral injury, which are similar and related, bear witness to the reality that we as human beings are not created to kill one another. In spite of all that the military presents itself to be—a means to education and job training, a way out of poverty, or something to do in order to find a life direction when you have none—the bottom line is that when a young person signs up for military service, she or he is agreeing to obey orders to kill whomever she or he is ordered to kill. For the young person who has been brought up in the Christian church, this decision is in conflict with Jesus' central teachings and the life to which he called and still calls people. The church largely has failed in its responsibility to talk openly and without apology with young people, their families, and the whole church about this most urgent moral decision. While there is admirable and important work going on to help those suffering from their participation in war, there needs to be work done at the "front end." Church leaders need to be raising the issue of military service and Christian conscience. This does not have to be done in a confrontational and judgmental way, but as a matter of taking seriously the teachings and life of Jesus as we make important moral decisions throughout our lives. Those who object even to the discussion of this issue, if they see themselves as Christian, must acknowledge the necessity of talking about moral decisions in light of Jesus' teachings, whether or not they are comfortable with it. Those who are most forcefully supportive of the military and military service need to recognize that they, too, as followers of Jesus, must in some way correlate their views and actions with the specific teachings of Jesus on nonviolence and love of enemies.

With the church in this society, there have always been, and are still, a number of elephants in the room, issues of human concern that are avoided. Human sexuality. Racism and white privilege. Continuing dominance of male leadership and the muting of women's voices and their exclusion from leadership. Among them all, however, I have found that the greatest silence has been surrounding the moral choice of whether or not to participate in the military and in war-making. As Christians, we seem always ready to acquiesce to the next war instigated by our nation. We seem always to give our silent or voiced approval and support to those who choose to be part of the killing. Yet, we seem unwilling to hold up to young people and adults the significance of choosing military service in the perspective of being followers of Jesus. We live in a nation led by those who are expanding military spending and actions, to the increasing neglect of the needs of our own country. There has never been a more urgent moment for followers of Jesus to examine themselves, their thoughts and their actions, in light of the one they have committed to follow, who teaches that the way of being a true human being, as we are created to be, does not include violence, war and killing.

11

Where Our Allegiance Lies

In recent times, the issue of whether or not one stands for the national anthem has arisen with a fury. There is also the companion matter of whether or not one repeats the "Pledge of Allegiance" to the flag, hand over heart. Perusing Facebook, one finds many posts vehemently defending the flag and its treatment, as though it is an entity in itself that demands our unquestioning adoration. These matters plunge us into the murky and turbulent waters of nationalism, of attachment to one's own country, its emblems and rituals. From our childhood, we have been trained to memorize words that state our supreme allegiance to a flag and to the "republic for which it stands." We have been forced to sing a national song that to most people is unsingable, with words strung together to conjure up images of battle. Militarism and war have become our culture's exclusive definers of patriotism. The teaching and sustaining of nationalism is woven so thoroughly into our culture that we accept it tacitly, without much, if any, critical thought.

What is religion's role in the perpetuation and fostering of nationalism in this country and, more specifically, in the churches? The national flag is found in most sanctuaries, unapologetically right up front, an unquestioned part of the furniture of our sacred spaces. We find many Sunday schools, Vacation Bible Schools, and preschool programs in which children are required to learn and say "the pledge." Stirring my faulty memory, I don't recall so much of this in my own background. I grew up in a middle-of-the-road Protestant denomination, in which my father was a minister. We did not perform any patriotic rites in summer church camps. There may have been a VBS here and there where the pledge was recited, likely followed by "The Lord's Prayer." Yet, even so, there was always a kind of shadowy presence of nationalistic sentiment coexisting with the gospel of "God so loved the world ..." I have learned since those early years growing up in the church that religion in the U.S. is thoroughly soaked in nationalism, in milder and more extreme forms.

We lived for many years in Lynchburg, Virginia, known most widely for the presence of Jerry Falwell's church, university and family. I watched Thomas Road Baptist Church as it outgrew an old orange juice company facility, steadily sprawling both in physical facilities and in membership. The church and Liberty University exemplified in the extreme our culture's marriage of God, nation and the military. The church sponsors "support the troops" and "celebrate America" events in which there is an abundance of nationalism and militarism, but nothing that one could perceive as Christian, in the sense of following the teachings or life of Jesus himself.

In the 1980s, Eberhard and Renate Bethge paid a visit to Lynchburg, made possible by their friendship with Dr. James Patrick Kelley, then on the religion faculty of Lynchburg College, a liberal arts college affiliated with the Christian Church (Disciples of Christ). Eberhard was the closest friend of Dietrich Bonhoeffer. Renate was Bonhoeffer's niece. While in the city, Eberhard was interested in visiting Thomas Road Baptist Church for worship. After doing so, he summed up the experience: "When the cross and the flag are placed side by side, the cross always loses." There could be no more perceptive observation than that, coming from one who lived through the rise and brutal reign of National Socialism in Germany. Beginning in the early 1930s, the German churches were quickly Nazified by appealing to nationalism and militarism already present in the churches. The cross, representing the life of love that is willing to suffer for the sake of others, loses out easily to the flag. In my own experience as a conscientious objector and a pastor, I have witnessed the visceral passion elicited by flag and gun, easily eclipsing the passion for following Jesus.

Allegiance means giving one's supreme loyalty to something or someone higher than oneself. It is a high-powered word. The biblical view is that there is no loyalty, allegiance, or, let us say, love, on a par with that owed to God. The preamble to the Decalogue, the Ten Commandments, is: "I am the Lord your God … you shall have no other gods before me." A god is anyone or anything we place beside or above God in our loyalties or allegiances. Yet, the facile joining of nationalism and religion says that you can, indeed, serve two gods. Love of God and love of nation are one allegiance. However, the heart of the Jewish/Christian tradition, and I suspect of other major religious traditions, says that this cannot be. For Christians, those would-be followers of Jesus' life and teachings, the flag cannot be placed beside the cross.

It is no wonder children growing into adulthood, having been nurtured in churches, encounter a significant spiritual struggle. Is it God, or nation? Or both? Where is my allegiance to be? We speak of the separation of church and state, or the non-establishment by the state of a particular religion. What we need today is a separation of state from church, the non-establishment of nationalism, along with militarism, in the church. The very tradition that lifts up supreme allegiance to God alone, beneath which all other loyalties or loves are to be examined and measured, at the same time speaks of God *and* country, cross *and* flag. We are imbedding in children and youth a terrible spiritual quandary which they eventually must untangle. At the same time, we are abandoning the one Great Allegiance of loving God with our whole being, as Jesus taught, the central business of the church.

The Jewish/Christian tradition, as well as other major spiritual traditions, opens us to the importance of an allegiance, or love, that is vast, full of mystery, and the source of lives filled with compassion, peace, joy, service to others, stewardship of the creation and all that makes us complete human beings, as we were created to be and to live. That allegiance nourishes wonder in our souls and saves us from the narrow, and often violent, prejudices of nation, race, social standing, gender, culture. Such an expansive love reveals to us the joy of living with material simplicity, avoiding the illusions of endless hunger for possession of things and the violence attending such pursuits. If we take our religious faith seriously enough to live with it over time, there grows in the heart and mind the sense of a Power and Presence infusing the whole of life, the love of which makes all other loyalties or allegiances of secondary value. And yet, that one Great Allegiance can lend to our other commitments and loyalties a necessary truth, mercy and humility. I have come to learn what allegiance means, and to know that mine is pledged to the everywhere presence of the Source and Power of Life, which we call God. I have learned this as a follower of Jesus. Others have learned it as followers of the Buddha, of the Prophet Muhammad, or as Lakota Native Americans experiencing God as Wakan Tanka. Because that Reality we call God is the source of all life, including my own. It is there that my Great Allegiance must lie. It is why I do not sing a nationalistic song or speak words of ultimate loyalty to a national flag. It is why, though my understanding was youthful and incomplete, I was clearly and strongly compelled to make my decision to be a conscientious objector. My allegiance lay with the everywhere-presence of God, a universal and compelling Love that is nonviolent at its core and in its essence.

Allegiance means giving our whole lives to something or someone. In the case of the Jewish/Christian tradition of spirituality, this means recognizing that our very lives, in their totality, belong to God alone. This was certainly the message of Jesus and the pattern of his life. When it comes to serving in the military, the issue becomes clear: To whom, or what, does my life belong? Can I give myself completely to a human institution that will demand that I kill others? Or, knowing that my life belongs completely and first to God, must I not refrain from participating in the military, war or war preparations, and killing those whose lives also belong first of all to God and not to me? We are meant to live by a greater allegiance than to flag and nation.

Especially in these days of crisis with regard to the environment, the very envelope of our own lives, we are learning that we belong to the Earth, the air, the water, the universe itself. This is the context in which we must consider our loyalties and our responsibilities.

Choosing Peace

A Discussion and Action Guide for **What Belongs to God**
By Kaye Edwards and Jason C. Stanley

Why Should We Discuss This Book?

This discussion and action guide is designed to spark self-examination and community action on peace-and-justice issues in today's world. So many urgent challenges are related to those issues, today, that you may wonder why we should think and talk about what it means to become a conscientious objector. One vital reason is to address the "unofficial draft" that channels many young people, especially in poor and marginalized communities, into the armed forces as one of the only career opportunities available to them. We can start with the question: Why are there so few alternatives? Why are we—as a country and as individuals—not creating more ways for people to serve our country, afford a college education and build a hopeful future without agreeing to participate in war?

The question of choosing peace, and objecting to war, also invites us to examine the many ways we, perhaps unknowingly, contribute to the lack of peace and justice within ourselves, our families, our communities and the wider world. In the words of Thich Nhat Hanh, "We often think of peace as the absence of war, that if powerful countries would reduce their weapon arsenals, we could have peace. But if we

look deeply into the weapons, we see our own minds—our own prejudices, fears and ignorance." (from *Living Buddha, Living Christ*)

By discussing this book, we will together find ways to promote
peace through the daily living of our own lives. Our congregations
can develop programs to help people of all ages find ways to serve
the community and the country that contribute to peace and serve
justice. We have written this guide hoping to foster a deeper understanding of ourselves and a greater awareness of the many ways we all
can encourage peace.

A last word from Thich Nhat Hanh, one of David's favorite writers:
"Our own life has to be our message" (from *The World We Have: A
Buddhist's Approach to Peace and Ecology*).

Let's Get Started

This discussion and action guide embodies the acronym PEACE,
a peacemaking process that is similar to a number of well-established
programs, including the Forum for Theological Exploration's CARE
practices and the Reuniting the Children of Abraham process, among
others. As you will find throughout this guide, we recommend that
you visit and connect with our website, WhatBelongsToGod.com,
where you will find additional resources you can download. We also
welcome your questions and news about events you are planning
related to this book.

P = Presence—Setting the Stage

E = Experiencing—Responding to the book

A = Awakening—Exploring personal stories related to the material

C = Connecting—Reflecting theologically

E = Enacting—Answering the question, "What now?"

Presence is setting the stage. It is about becoming focused in the
present moment, through a prayer, a song and some silence. Consider
having a worship table and a group covenant. If you do not already

have a group covenant, and want to create one, we are providing more information that you can download for free on our website.

Experiencing is how we respond to the book. Summaries of the chapters could contain questions that might trigger a conversation. For example, "Are we in conflict or agreement with particular statements? How so?" If you are prioritizing the most important questions for your group, some questions and insights could be put in a "parking lot," like a large sheet of newsprint used to store and remember key issues you may not be able to explore in depth at the time.

Awakening is an invitation, through a few simple questions, to explore personal stories related to the material. These questions are open-ended, usually starting with "what" or "how" and are short in length. Beginning questions with, "I wonder," is a good way to put people at ease: "I wonder, can you tell us more?" To do the work of peace and justice "out there," we must find safe spaces to examine ourselves and tell our own stories. It is important to be an active listener. When we are actively listening, our focus is on the storyteller, listening with wonder and curiosity. Stories approached with wonder and curiosity can bring about important awakenings for both the listener and the storyteller.

Connecting is the critical and theological reflection needed for peacemaking. We do this by exploring sacred writings mentioned in the book and modern-day sages, scholars and saints who teach and guide us in efforts of peacemaking in our time. These reflections can inform and shape a more faithful understanding of peace and justice and the actions we take in its pursuit, no matter our faith tradition.

Enacting is seeking to answer the question, "Now what?" The book has been read, a fruitful discussion has taken place—now what? This process invites our imaginations to create a plan for promoting peace and justice in our personal lives, our communities and beyond. Brainstorming allows creativity. The enacting might take the form of a community action that the group does together, or that an individual does alone. As justice often moves us beyond comfort zones, it can raise resentments. It is important to reflect on and discuss the boundaries of comfort zones and any resentments. They just might inspire a new work of peace and justice. This is a very personal journey that never ends and can lead to a whole new way of life for some of us. Learning more about the causes of poverty might turn into a permanent volunteer job in a food pantry; helping to organize a protest may bring more diversity into one's social circle. Maybe parenting methods will change. Maybe negative thinking about oneself will change.

Options for Using this Guide

The material presented here is designed for a three-day, two-night retreat. However, the guide can be adapted for a one-day workshop or a more comprehensive study for multiple weeks. If done as a one-day workshop, we recommend planning for a five to six hour day. If working with a large group, it might be helpful to break into smaller groups for some of the discussions and activities. When using these materials in a weekly schedule, the retreat's Friday night session becomes Week 1, the Saturday morning session is Week 2, and the Saturday afternoon is Week 3. The Sunday session is Week 4.

For all options, begin the first session with a welcome and introductions. Begin by talking about the author, David Livingston Edwards. David's wife, Kaye, provides an introduction in the book that you may want to use. Consider defining together terms like conscientious objector, draft, peace, non-violence and justice. You could visit our website and share the PEACE-acronym handout with your group.

Helpful supplies

You will want to find your own:

- Bibles
- Markers, crayons, pens and pencils
- White paper, red paper and newsprint
- Sticky notes
- Play dough
- Blue tape

From our website WhatBelongsToGod.com, you can get:

- Samples of David Edwards' music
- Handouts including a thermometer chart, an example covenant, a story writing worksheet, a plan to promote peace and justice—and the PEACE-acronym overview. As we hear from readers, we plan to add other resources as well, so please do connect with us online.

From Wikipedia, you can get:

- Picture of the sculpture "Let Us Beat Swords into Plowshares" by Evgeniy Vuchetich: https://en.wikipedia.org/wiki/Yevgeny_Vuchetich

RETREAT: Friday Night

Remember, you could adapt this program into a weekly series. This session works best over about three hours. Here is the outline we recommend, organized around the PEACE process.

Presence (5 minutes)

Play David's recording of "Blessed Are the Peacemakers" (*Arabella's Eyes, track #5, whatbelongstogod.com/music/AE-Peacemakers.mp3*). After the song, spend a few moments in silence.

Prayer. You could use: "O God, who dwells within each of us, we give thanks for this day. We gather in this space to hear the stories of your servants. Open our ears, hearts, and minds as we explore what it means to be an objector to war, a peacemaker, and a conscientious objector in our time. God of Peace, help us to respond to all violence with peace and justice for all people. May our time together guide us to be servants of compassion and justice for a more peaceful world. Amen."

Experiencing (20 minutes)

This is a chance for everyone in the group to become familiar with the wide range of reactions the book may evoke. We hope that all participants will have read it in advance. Then, this "Experiencing" time gives everyone a sense of how the whole book affected readers sitting in the room around them. Invite the sharing of highlights from each chapter. Summarize, then encourage the sharing of feelings or emotions. Pay particular attention to any areas where people seem to find conflict with something David wrote and gently explore those areas by asking, "Can you tell us about why you felt conflict with that part of the book?"

Awakening (30 minutes)

Discuss the intersection of David's story with our own experiences using the questions below. Listen to each other with open hearts and ask additional questions, making sure that everyone who wishes to speak is heard.

- Tell a story of how you or a family member responded to the draft. What impact did it have on you and your family?
- David talks about Mr. Clarence Parker, a high school social studies teacher, who challenged David into a "wake-up call" (Chapter 1). Have any of you had wake-up calls or "aha-moment" experiences when it comes to peace and justice?
- The Rev. Herb R. Moore played an essential role in helping David with his conscientious objector application, as well as his more robust understanding of peace and non-violence (Chapter 5). Who in your life plays a critical role in your sense of peace and justice? Tell us about that person.
- From an essay by Paul A. Rieman, David experienced a "wake-up call" with the Cain and Abel story in Genesis 4. He writes about this experience in Chapter 2. Have you ever had an experience with scripture like that? Tell us about it.
- Think about a time when you experienced punishment over compassion. I wonder what impact this experience had on you?

Before taking a break, consider praying this prayer, "O God, remind us that you made us in your image. Look with compassion on the whole human family; take away the arrogance and hatred which infect our hearts. Break down the walls that separate us and unite us in bonds of love, so we may work through our struggle and confusion to accomplish your purposes on earth; that, in your good time, all nations and races may serve you in harmony. Amen." (Adapted from the prayer "For the Human Family." *The Book of Common Prayer.*)

Connecting (40 minutes)

Throughout the book, David looks to Jesus as an example of a nonviolent presence. He often refers to Jesus' Sermon on the Mount (Matthew 4:23-7:29). In some editions of the Bible, the words of Jesus have been printed in red to elevate their importance. Yet, many of these "red letters," as David points out, run counter to cultural Christianity.

We will take a closer look at some of the scriptures David cites in chapter 6: Matthew 5:9, Matthew 5:23-26, and Matthew 5:43-48. As we read the texts together—and review what David has to say about these passages in the book—discuss what impact these verses may have on our efforts to promote peace and non-violence. On a red sheet of paper, to remind us of the blood that has been shed by the violence in our community and beyond, write one take-away from the scripture that is essential to promote peace and justice. Tape the red sheet to the wall.

If your group is large, divide into smaller groups, each taking one scripture. After about 15-20 minutes, bring the groups together and invite them to share their take-aways. Tape the red sheets to a wall.

Enacting (60 minutes)

As the work of actually being a peacemaker begins, we need to share our stories and experiences with peace, non-violence and justice. Using the Story Writing worksheet available online, write about a "wake-up call" as David describes it, or write about the desire for a yet to happen "wake-up call."

Encourage participants to take their worksheet and pen to a comfortable spot. As everyone gathers back, they may be in a different emotional and spiritual place depending on the story they just wrote. Invite the group to pair up and share their stories with a partner. Encourage the listeners to listen without asking questions until the storyteller finishes. Then, ask questions, such as "I wonder if you can say more about ..." or "I'm curious about ... ." End this session with a short prayer.

RETREAT: Saturday morning (approximately 2 hours)

Presence (15 minutes)

Look at the picture of the sculpture "Let Us Beat Swords into Plow-shares" by Evgeniy Vuchetich, which stands outside of the United Nations Building in New York. When you look at this sculpture, what comes to mind? What does it invoke in you? Read Isaiah 2:2-4.

Invite the group to be in silent prayer.

Then, lead a group prayer for peace, perhaps from a denominational resource book available to you. Most denominations have a rich array of resources that local congregations can access. For example, we especially like the "Litany for Peace with Justice Sunday" found in *The United Methodist Book of Worship*. Look around and you are likely to discover other similar Protestant and Catholic prayers that are available for your group to reproduce and share.

Experiencing (10 minutes)

Using the crayons and paper, construct pictures of Jesus before the wake-up call to peace and justice as shared in Session 1. Be sensitive to the wide range of artistic abilities in any group and the likelihood that some people may be hesitant to jump into this hands-on exercise. Encourage everyone to create an image of Jesus before a "wake-up call" or a desire for a "wake-up call." Invite participants to share their pictures and ask questions.

Awakening (20 minutes)

This book captures the tension between a God of punishment and a God of compassion. Cultural Christianity wants us to understand God through the lens of discipline instead of the kindness we experience through Jesus. Recall insights gained from Chapters 9-11. David discusses some hard truths in Chapter 9, yet essential truths to wrestle with to promote peace and justice. Spend a few moments discussing what some of us might have wrestled with when reading these chapters. I wonder how our egos get in the way of living as followers of Jesus? What are we giving to the emperor that belongs to God?

Connecting (40 minutes)

During Solomon's reign, the struggle for Israel changed from the conquest of the land to the conquest of the soul. As the focus on the temple arose, a challenging relationship replaced Israel's faithful relationship with God. It is during this time that the prophets rise to declare the people's unfaithfulness.

Give each person some play dough and choose one of these three scriptures: Amos 5:21-24, Hosea 10:14-15, Micah 4:1-5. After reading the scripture, mold the play dough into something representing the vision of peace and justice heard in the scripture. All are invited to share their play dough creations and what they symbolize. Our understanding of God influences how we understand peace and justice. Looking at the symbols we have created, what do they tell us about who God is, and how we know peace and justice?

Jesus taught his disciples that they need to reexamine what is important. What culture and society tell us is important does not always align with Jesus' teachings, which speaks to the tension of giving to the emperor what belongs to God. Read Mathew 22:15-22. Since reading David's book, how do we read these verses differently? Does this new reading change our understanding of God? If so, how?

While teaching in seminary, the German theologian Dietrich Bonhoeffer had a wake-up call in his spiritual life thanks to Jesus' Sermon on the Mount. There was a tension between the comfortable Christianity of privilege he was experiencing and Jesus' call to discipleship. Bonhoeffer concludes that Christians and Christian communities are to live as Christ's first followers. As such, discipleship's cost is to live outside of our comfort and privilege and live as Christ would. If we embrace the cost of discipleship as Bonhoeffer did, what needs to change in our lives? What are the biggest challenges to living as followers of Jesus and being peacemakers in our current reality?

Enacting (40 minutes)

Our response to a loving, peaceful, and just God is to be loving, peaceful and just to ourselves and others. This understanding may place new importance on how we each individually and collectively live our lives and make decisions.

Consider visiting our website and using the "Take Your Peace-making Temperature" handout as a self-assessment. At the bottom of the thermometer is "Unknowing," which means not recognizing a problem. "Curious" is acknowledging what others have done in peacemaking, leaving you wondering what it would mean for you to do such work. "Awareness" is being aware of injustices. "Gestures" are acts like collecting socks for the homeless or sending money to an organization. "Engagement" means getting involved in justice work by such things as volunteering and building relationships with people who are oppressed, calling out racism, aligning oneself with peace-makers, learning about white privilege. "Systemic change" is asking why systems are unjust and asking, "What can I do to bring about change?"

We color in the thermometer to the level that best represents our peacemaking. If participants fill out this sheet individually, then share them with each other, we are likely to see a wide range of tempera-tures represented. This is a rich opportunity for discussion.

Read the last paragraph of Chapter 4. These words beg us to ask ourselves, "What are we going to do about the killings and the murders?" To answer that question, we first need to name current injustices. Prepare for this next step in the discussion by posting a large piece of paper with three columns, labeled, Our Lives, Our Community and Our Nation. Invite your group to call out injustices and situations in which peace is challenged. Now that the current realities of injustice and lack of peace have been named, brainstorm ideas for promoting peace and justice. Write one idea per sticky note, then post it on the wall. Remember that, when brainstorming, there are no bad ideas. Every idea is a valued contribution to the discussion. As people finish, invite them to walk around and look at the different sticky notes. Encourage them to ask themselves, "What do I notice? Which ideas do I appreciate? Are there additional possibilities?"

If you want to work on a group plan, begin grouping similar sticky notes together, placing them in a horizontal row from left to right. As duplicates or similar ideas appear, stick these sticky notes below the ones representing the same idea. When completed, it will be easy to see the top ideas, as they will have the most extended vertical presence. Have some discussion about the top 5 ideas and determine which are priorities for the group. Write down the ideas considered to be a priority for an action plan. What other action steps are needed? Write action steps on sticky notes and arrange in sequential order. Team up and talk through plans.

RETREAT: Saturday afternoon (approximately 2 hours)

Presence (10 minutes)

Read Matthew 19:13-15. Play David's song, "What Will We Say to the Children?" (*What Will We Say to the Children?*, track #9, whatbelongstogod. com/music/AE-Winds.mp3). Spend time in silent mediation asking, "What will we say to the children?"

Experiencing (20 minutes)

Recall the experience of reading Chapters 7 and 8.

Awakening (30 minutes)

In the book, David acknowledges that when we decide to promote peace and non-violence, others may not understand or may try to justify violence by using Jesus' words. He writes in Chapter 7, "Such decisions can and almost certainly will bring us into conflict with those things and people which lay claim to our loyalties."

As we consider the plans that we are developing to promote peace and justice, what are the obstacles? As obstacles are named, write each one on a sheet of newsprint. Then, for each barrier, list ideas for addressing that concern.

What organizations or individuals can we identify as allies in our peacemaking? Similarly, list allies on newsprint and generate ideas for inviting these allies to join in your efforts.

Connecting (20 minutes)

In the New Testament, children began to run up to Jesus. However, they were stopped by the disciples, based on the cultural understanding that children occupied a low rung on the social ladder. Children were not to bother the rabbi. Jesus, however, changed the narrative. Read Mark 9:33-37. Jesus' disciples had their priorities all wrong, even after spending so much time with Jesus. By taking a child on his knee, Jesus taught his disciples that they needed to reexamine what was important and focus on those on the social ladder's lower rungs. I wonder if/how our priorities might have changed during this experience?

Enacting (30-40 minutes)

At this point, your group will have generated a list of ideas that could be put into action. Possible obstacles have been named and discussed. Potential allies have been identified. Now the action steps can be named that will help promote peace and justice, one that aligns with our understanding of God and is as free of ego as we can make it.

If you visit our website, you can use the "My Plan to Promote Peace and Justice" handout to organize your plans. We are ready to begin sharing these plans with others.

As we have mentioned before, adapt this outline to the size of your group. Perhaps you want to divide a larger group to give more people a chance to speak in smaller circles. End the session with a prayer.

RETREAT: Sunday (approximately 2 hours)

Presence (10 minutes)

In the online description of the song "Winds of Change," (*Arabella's Eyes, track #1, whatbelongstogod.com/music/AE-Winds.mp3*) David says, "I wrote 'Winds of Change' April 16, 2007, the morning after a terrible spring storm, and the wind was still wild. I was staying at a friend's lake house at Smith Mountain Lake in Virginia. The electricity was off, and public radio on my battery-powered radio was a little scratchy out there, but I could make out reports coming from Virginia Tech, where 32 students and faculty died in a mass shooting. I kept working on the song, and by the time I finished, it had a whole new meaning for me."

Experiencing (20 minutes)

In an earlier session, we constructed a picture of Jesus before a wake-up call, or a desire for such a call, to peace and justice. When we look at our drawings, how has that image of Jesus changed during this retreat? Use the markers to make changes or create new images of Jesus.

Awakening (15 minutes)

In Chapter 7, we read about David being accosted by others because of his understanding of peace, non-violence and justice. We are about to implement our plans to promote peace and justice. There may be people who will see this commitment very differently than we do. What concerns do we have about the plan's reception? What are ways we can support one another as we implement the plans?

Connecting (20 minutes)

Read Micah 6:6-8. Are there any new insights we have gained through this experience of reading this book. Do we now answer differently the question, "What does the Lord require of us?"

Enacting (10 minutes)

Consider asking everyone in the group to say a one- or two-word blessing for going forth, remembering that the work of peace and justice is ongoing.

Together, recite the Prayer of St. Francis.

Lord, make me an instrument of your peace
Where there is hatred, let me sow love
Where there is injury, pardon
Where there is doubt, faith

Where there is despair, hope
Where there is darkness, light
And where there is sadness, joy
O Divine Master, grant that I may
Not so much seek to be consoled as to console
To be understood, as to understand
To be loved, as to love
For it is in giving that we receive
And it's in pardoning that we are pardoned
And it's in dying that we are born to Eternal Life

Amen.

About the Study Guide's Co-Author:
the Rev. Jason C. Stanley

The Rev. Jason C. Stanley is an ordained deacon in the United Methodist Church, committed to helping churches see and address the needs of justice and compassion in their communities. For over 20 years, Jason has served in churches as a layperson and ordained clergy in ministry with children and youth and their families. He now serves as district staff for the Elizabeth River District in Virginia.

Jason holds a Masters in Christian Education from Union Presbyterian Seminary in Richmond, Virginia. He has contributed to curriculum resources including a curriculum that accompanies the Rev. Dr. Michael W. Waters' book *Stakes is High* (Chalice Press) and to the Faith & Justice youth curriculum produced by the General Board of Church and Society of the United Methodist Church.

Jason, and his wife the Rev. Megan Saucier, and their two beautiful daughters, live in Norfolk, Virginia. You can find Jason at JasonCStanley.com.

About the Author: David L. Edwards

Esophageal cancer may have diminished David's ability to sing and speak before finally taking his life on March 4, 2019, but it did not take away his gentle loving spirit or voice. He lives on through his commitment to peace and justice and continues to speak through the written word and his music.

David inherited his love of music from his parents, who hailed from Appalachian Southwest Virginia, where music flows throughout worship, fun and all of life. Though this book is only his second published work, he was a prolific writer of sermons, essays, poetry and music.

David attended Lynchburg College (now the University of Lynchburg) in Lynchburg, Virginia and Lexington Theological Seminary in Lexington, Kentucky. His alternative service to the draft was performed as an orderly on the cardiac ward of Boston Children's Hospital, Boston, Massachusetts. During his career as a minister, he served congregations in Kentucky, Indiana and Virginia. David is greatly missed by his family, his wife of 50 years, his two adult children and three grandchildren, one of whom was born 10 months after his death. He loved fishing, hiking the Blue Ridge Mountains and swimming in the ocean, and singing, especially with children. A kinder, more peace-loving man would be hard to find.

David contributed in many ways to what is good in this world, and he believed that the most important witness of his life was his decision to be a Conscientious Objector during the Vietnam War. *What Belongs to God* not only reveals the story of his decision and its legacy, but shows how David tells the story as an invitation to readers to discover the ways we all are called to be peacemakers.

I hope you enjoy and are challenged by this book and David's music. You may contact me through the website, www.whatbelongstogod. com, where you will also find a free download of David's music and study guide resources.

Peace,

Kaye Edwards

WhatBelongsToGod@gmail.com

We would be remiss to not acknowledge our mother's tireless efforts to fulfill our father's wishes with the publication of this book following his earthly departure. *What Belongs to God* was penned by our father, however, was co-authored by our loving mother, Kaye; not just with her diligent efforts completing publication, but as his life partner. This is his story and collectively their experience. They were the source of each other's strength.

Love always,

Kent and Shelley

More Books About Peacemaking

Find these books on Amazon.com, Barnesandnoble.com, Walmart.com and other retailers. eBook formats available.

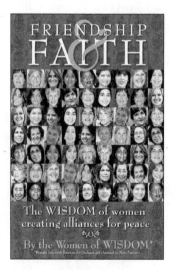

Friendship & Faith: The WISDOM of women creating alliances for peace

by the Women of WISDOM

Making a new friend often is tricky, as you'll discover in these dozens of real-life stories by women from a wide variety of religious and ethnic backgrounds. But, crossing lines of religion, race and culture is worth the effort, often forming some of life's deepest friendships.

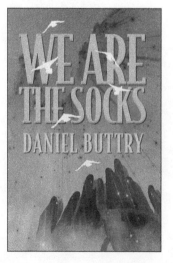

We Are The Socks

by Daniel Buttry

Every day, we hear news from around the world about war and violence. The idea of peacemaking seems impossible—unless you're Daniel Buttry. An ordained minister and seasoned peacemaker, Dan has traveled to some of the most dangerous places in the world to conduct conflict resolution, train clergy and elders, and transform conflict into peace.

Find these books on Amazon.com, Barnesandnoble.com, Walmart.com and other retailers. eBook formats available.

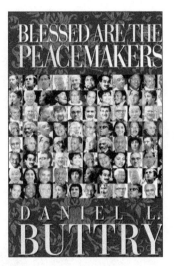

Blessed Are The Peacemakers

by Daniel Buttry

In the pages of this book, you will meet more than 100 heroes, but most of them are not the kind of heroes our culture celebrates for muscle, beauty and wealth. These are peacemakers. They circle the planet. A few are famous like Gandhi and Bono of U2, but most of them you will discover for the first time in these stories.

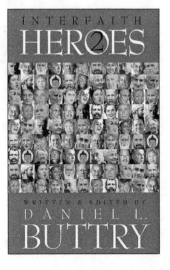

Interfaith Heroes 1 & Interfaith Heroes 2

by Daniel Buttry

Join peacemaker Daniel Buttry as he profiles interfaith heroes and peacemakers from around the world and throughout history. Learn how these peace innovators mediated conflict and transformed their communities.